EMAILS FROM INDIA

WOMEN WRITE HOME

EMAILS FROM INDIA

WOMEN WRITE HOME

EDITED BY JANIS HARPER

Seraphim
EDITIONS

The publisher gratefully acknowledges the financial assistance of the Canada Council for the Arts.

Canada Council   Conseil des arts
for the Arts   du Canada

Library and Archives Canada Cataloguing in Publication

    Emails from India : women write home / edited by Janis Harper.

ISBN 978-1-927079-21-8 (pbk.)

    1. Women--Travel--India. 2. Women travelers--India--Correspondence. 3. Women--Canada--Correspondence. 4. India--Description and travel. I. Harper, Janis, 1960-, editor of compilation

DS414.2.E43 2013   915.404'532   C2013-905090-6

In-House Editor: Kathryn McKeen
Design and Typography: Rolf Busch
Interior Art: Andhra Pradesh, India, and Map of India by Mariken Van Nimwegen

Published in 2013 by
Seraphim Editions
54 Bay Street
Woodstock, ON
Canada N4S 3K9

Printed and bound in Canada

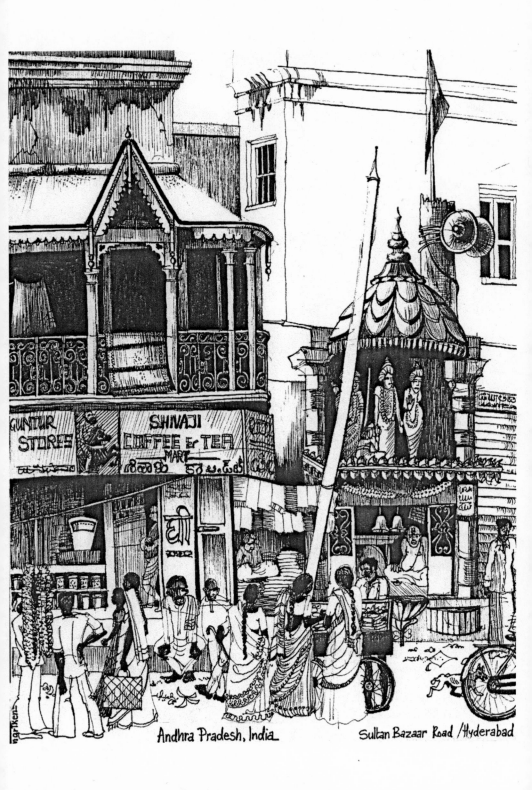

Andhra Pradesh, India   Sultan Bazaar Road / Hyderabad

CONTENTS

RAJASTHAN

En route

MUMBAI

En route

KOLKATA

THE SOUTH

GOA

En route

PREFACE

I'm in love with India. I don't know what it is about her, really. Of course, one could go on and on about her many accomplishments, her wisdom, spirituality, beauty. India is fascinating, complicated and attractive. But that's not really it. Our connection is more mystical, mysterious, ineffable. I know there are many like me who are drawn to her – at first, perhaps, because of our interest in religion or art or history, but then we find our interest flaming into passion. And if we're lucky enough to go there and meet her, we either deepen our connection or break it off immediately and return home, confused and bewildered. India is a place of extremes, and she brings them out in us. She challenges us, our perceptions about ourselves and the world, appearance and reality.

My love story with India began when I was a teenager and interested in eastern religions. When I began to travel in my twenties, backpacker style, India was always my ultimate destination. But I never made it there. There always seemed to be some obstacle. Then I settled down in my hometown of Vancouver, Canada, got married, had a family and a career, and had to satisfy myself with being an Indophile. I told myself I would make it to India by the time I turned fifty, but I could not foresee it happening. My divorce a few years ago changed that. The life-structures that I'd built over a long period of time suddenly collapsed, and through the opening created, I took myself to India. For seven weeks, I travelled alone and in a way that I hadn't done since my twenties. My appetite for India only grew, and the following year I took my sixteen-year-old son out of grade eleven, and we travelled together in India for three months. I turned fifty the following year. And India isn't done with me yet.

Women and India have always had a special relationship. For some reason, women like to travel in India – often alone – and have been doing so since the time of the British Raj. When I encounter women who have been drawn to India, it's obvious that we share a bond; we have been initiated into a special and wondrous sisterhood. We immediately want to share our stories with each other – not just for practical reasons, but also for pleasure and a sense of community.

After I'd returned from India, a woman I'd never met before approached me on the street and told me how much she enjoyed my emails from India. This continued to happen – women who knew that I was a friend of a friend (of a friend) told me that my emails were passed on to her, and she had passed them on to her friends. I had no idea that my emails were circulating in this way. I, too, found myself reading emails from India written by women I'd never met, passed on to me by people who thought I'd be interested. I was, very much so. The idea for this book was born.

Although *Emails from India* is not a traditional travel guide with how-to-get-there and where-to-go-and-stay information, it serves a similar purpose. It shows you how you can get there and where you might want to go, only it does so through the telling of personal experiences: approaching the Nepalese border on the night bus from New Delhi, meditating at the Beatles' Ashram in Rishikesh, being an extra in a television commercial in Mumbai, teaching yoga in Kerala and setting up to film a documentary in the northern village of Bansi. There are stories from the streets of the big cities, the touristy beaches of Goa, the less-travelled places and, of course, the trains and buses. Like emails, many of these pieces provoke a sense of immediacy, as if you're reading the words of someone who is there right *now*. Although the contents are structured according to place, one can also just leaf through the book, reading this and that, and not feel bogged down by linear progression. This collection is meant to be reminiscent of emails, something that one has an easy and in-the-moment relationship with.

I would have liked to have read this book before I travelled in India that first time, and I know that my future journeys there will be enriched by what is in these pages. If I'd had a book like this as a companion on my journeys, I would have felt part of the community of women travellers in India, sharing similar experiences, learning from the wisdom of my sisters, instead of feeling, at times, alone and over-whelmed. So many of us, especially those of us travelling on our own, can fall prey to our own distrust and suspicion in situations involving local men or money, and our fear of being taken advantage of can blind us to the beauty and the (usually) non-threatening reality around us. This book is a remedy to that: it builds a bright road on which a woman can meet India head-on, instead of with downcast eyes on the side paths, avoiding her, being too careful.

There are themes here that speak to our common experiences. For example, as women travellers in India we can't help but run into the prevalent attitude towards western women, and several of these stories explore this, sometimes with humour – like Leanne Leduc's tale of sharing a night train compartment with a lascivious man and Jasmine Yen's account of a creative advance from a would-be suitor. And there are themes common to all India travellers: the food, the smells, the poverty, the distinct gender roles, the ubiquitous con artists, the exuberant children underfoot and in your heart, and the spirituality in all of its many shapes and guises.

There are the challenges of getting from here to there, and the patience, the art of waiting, that we learn to cultivate as we adapt to abrupt changes in schedules, endless tangles of red tape, broken-down vehicles – in short, the many faces of the unforeseen, as numerous as the gods of Hinduism. As Vawn Himmelsbach tells us, "[Y]ou're forced to pay attention, to be aware, to live in the moment. . . . India is full of unexpected twists and turns, whether it's a bus trip or a journey inward." And Mariken Van Nimwegen writes about learning how to "just wait" in the face of the unexpected: "It's one of life's important ego-busting tests. It also manages to stretch your senses, check your opinions and self-knowledge, reach out to the 'other' world around you, a world where faith and karma still rule." India will take you where you want to go, but you have to let her. India has taught many of us lessons in trust.

Emails From India is not just for women. It's for anyone who has felt the allure of India, or who has been touched by India in some way. I hope that it instils dreams of India in those who have never been and nostalgia in those who have. I hope it educates and intrigues those who are planning a journey there. And I hope that it helps draw a map of compelling places to visit for those who have this book tucked into their backpacks. Ultimately, I hope that the voices in these pages speak to you and take you with them. Welcome to our India.

– Janis Harper, Vancouver, B.C.

En route

Subject: Welcome to India

From: Kathryn Sutton

"Welcome to India!" said the friendly young soldier at the Mumbai airport, looking me over a tad too thoroughly and then waving me off with his enormous, taped-together AK-47 and a smile. Strangely, my boyfriend, Andy, didn't get the same warm greeting.

However, the "western woman" novelty ended when everyone started deferring to my "husband" even when I spoke to them directly. Case in point. I booked the hotel. I paid for the hotel. I walked into the hotel and told them as much. The old man behind the desk turned to Andy and said "Sir? How long will you be staying?" Same deal at the restaurant. And in the cab. And at the bloody internet café I'm at now. Ah yes, this is going to be one big exercise in humility and humour. Any bets on which one gives out first?

India is already full of excitement. In the past thirty-six hours, I have met Miss World, Bollywood legend Anil Kapoor, and a man who appeared to be only a torso speaking to me from the gutter. I have seen palaces and slums (more of the latter than the former), stepped in human excrement and been an extra in a Bollywood movie. (*Salaam e Ishqe* – keep your eyes on your local listings.) It has been many things, but boring isn't one of them.

We're heading down the coast in a few days. In the meantime, don't worry about us. We're safe and sound and living like kings.

I'm a Celebrity. Get Me Out of Here.

What was I saying about wanting people to talk to me? I take it all back. Being a blonde, white woman in Hampi is sort of like being a celebrity at a movie premiere but without the velvet ropes.

We arrived in Hampi, Karnataka, on the final day of a huge Hindu festival. People had come from all over the country to take part in the event, which, to an outside observer, seemed to involve little more than watching a statue of a bull being dipped in a mouldy pond. Clearly, I'm not grasping much of the cultural context of it though. While it might sound mundane, the intensity of the whole event was otherworldly. I'm at a loss as to how to describe the chaos.

Next to the wet bull, I was the major attraction. Nearly every man I passed – all three million of them or so – either

a) tried to "accidentally" bump me;

b) ogled me;

c) asked to "make picture" with me;

or, more often than not,

d) did all of the above.

The attention is going to be hard to get used to.

The last week or so has been mostly temples and ruins punctuated by children asking for "school pen, chocolate, rupee" – always those three things and always in that order. While riding bikes down a hill, we even heard one kid wail "schoooool pennnnnnn" as we whizzed past him. The kids here seem much better off than in other places we've been, but it's their determination that really sets them apart.

We're heading to the beach tonight on one of India's infamous night buses. They're not particularly fast or comfortable, but they are mostly safe and ludicrously cheap. I have a feeling this won't be our last ride on one. I must be some sort of masochist. Next up: Gokarna. It's a hard life.

I'll be Home for Christmas (if only in my dreams)

It's Christmas in Gokarna: the holy cows have donned their Santa hats, the street kids burst into the occasional rendition of "Go Tell it on the Mountain," and cheer and merriment are in the air. Or is that just the smell of dung? I find it hard to tell these days.

This south of India is surprisingly Catholic, so Christmas celebrations are in full swing. Around these parts, you're just as likely to see a roadside idol of Mother Mary as you are of Vishnu or any of the other more popular Hindu gods. In fact, with their matching marigold offerings, it's often hard to tell which is which. One of my favourite things about India is how so many cultures and religions all live cheek-by-jowl in relative harmony. Not an easy feat when there are a billion of you stuffed into a country.

Please have a piece of Tofurkey and a stiff drink for me. I will most likely be constructing a Christmas tree out of sand and seashells tomorrow.

Goa-n and Try It

We're up in Goa to get in touch with our inner aging hippies. It's hot, there are stray cows and dogs everywhere, and the rats are the size of beagles. In short, we're having a wonderful time.

The infamous western burn-outs are here in force though. Yesterday we went to a beach party in Colva, which was pretty much made up exclusively of middle-aged, sunburned British expats singing "Mustang Sally" off-key while waving sparklers around. The legendary Goa party scene is very much dead and buried.

Regardless, the sun, surf and nearly free beer are keeping us going strong. We're heading up to Anjuna tomorrow to load up on tiny soapstone statues of Vishnu (guess what you're getting as souvenirs?), after which we'll head to Kerala for more cows, rats and maybe a little backwater house boating. I can't wait!

Wangs Galore in Bangalore

We're in Bangalore, soaking up the sun, sights and the occasional flasher. I'm thinking of setting up some sort of charitable trust with the aim of fostering peaceful, respectful and friendly relations between Indian men and foreign women. Either that or I'm going to start wearing a Margaret Thatcher mask. Not to worry though. Nothing truly scary or upsetting has happened, and I seriously doubt it will. So far, India strikes me as a very law-abiding country. Women travellers just need to have a thick skin when it comes to oglers. Mine is toughening up by the minute.

Over-excited men aside, Bangalore could have been any other city in the world, with its endless coffee chains (Barista beats Café Coffee Day hands down, if you're interested), pubs and towering glass skyscrapers. The highlight of our stay was a bar called Pub World that crammed a western saloon, German bar, Manhattan club and English pub into one room. It took us half an hour to figure out which section we were in, but it was lovely (if expensive) to have Guinness.

Valentine's Day Indian-Style

Who would have known that a few heart-shaped candies and plush toys could cause so much fuss? Yesterday, extremist Hindu groups held protests against Valentine's Day celebrations across the country, owing to the fact that V-Day is a foreign festival that corrupts traditional values. Mostly the protests were contained to burning cards, but apparently some couples were assaulted. Yikes. Andy and I spent the day safe from the hardliners because we were recovering from a joint case of food poisoning. Now that's romance!

In other news, we're in Pondicherry, which is one of my favourite Indian towns so far. It was formerly a French colony so the food here is an amazing mash-up of French and South Indian fabulousness. I could happily stay here and gorge myself for the rest of the trip.

It's also a vaguely odd town. Much of Pondicherry seems to be run by a local international community called Auroville, which has a very cult-like feel to it. We went to visit their ashram and discovered they make really tasty French food (so, cult or not, they're fine by me!). However, we were disappointed they wouldn't let us look at their giant crystal, which their followers say is the biggest in the world. Everything seems to have a connection to Auroville here. Even our hotel room has a picture in it of the spiritual leader (known simply as "The Mother"). I swear she follows me with her eyes. Spooky.

Lions and Tigers and Bears – Oh My!

We've just returned from the wilds of Bandhavgarh National Park in Madhya Pradesh. We went there to spot tigers in the wild, and boy did we ever! Five of them! Two were even cubs (though, I'll admit, very big cubs). Clearly, this trip has aggravated me at times, but it has been worthwhile for the tigers alone. They were absolutely breathtaking! I think I'll be riding high on this for a while.

We're now in Khajuraho, the City of Temples. The temples around here are probably the best we've seen so far (and are widely regarded to be the best examples of Indian temple sculpture). They're covered in all sorts of dirty Kamasutra-style images. It's kind of awesome. It's particularly funny to see how many elderly tourists have come from all over the globe to see what amounts to ancient porn. One of the sculptures looks exactly like Paris Hilton and is even carrying a little dog like she always does. I'll send pictures at some point. The resemblance is uncanny.

Agra-vation

Agra – home of the Taj Mahal – is a funny city. Not really "Funny Ha-Ha" but more "Funny I'm-Going-To-Kill-Someone." We'd been warned that this city was India's centre of tourist hassle, but we didn't really think it would be different than any major city. Boy, were we wrong.

The rickshaw drivers are menacing, the dogs howl their haunting canine symphony from dusk until dawn, and the teenage boys seem to have a barely contained hostility cracking just below the surface. It's an unpleasant combination of maddening and, for the first time on this trip, downright frightening. We leave at 6:00 AM tomorrow.

The Taj Mahal, however, really does live up to the hype. Pictures really can't do it justice. The way the light hits it is surreal. Sort of like a Disney movie on steroids. You have to see it for yourself, although I'll be sure to bring everyone a tiny plastic replica of the place!

The past few weeks have been eventful, to say the least. Varanasi is definitely not for the squeamish, what with the daily cremations taking place on the riverbank of the Ganges, but it is a fascinating and beautiful place. We left town, via train, just two days before terrorists blew the station up. Unfortunately, this isn't the first time Andy and I have found ourselves in the middle of terrorist violence. I never have anything eloquent to say about it. It is just infuriating and heartbreaking. Needless to say, we are fine, and our trip goes on as planned.

We're off to Rajasthan tomorrow for a little camel trekking and then up to Punjab to see the Golden Temple.

Hope you're all well. Let me know if I can make an offering for any of you (please specify religion, problem and favourite god) – what's ten rupees among friends?

Hello Dalai!

We're in McLeod Ganj now with what seems to be every Buddhist, boomer and hippie on the planet. We managed to accidentally time our visit with the Dalai Lama's annual public lectures, so we're working on getting security clearance to see him (let's hope Andy's mafia past won't rear its ugly head yet again!). However, our auspicious timing was a real pain in the ass when we had to schlep our stuff all over town to find a room during a hailstorm last night. After all these months in the sun, I'd forgotten what cold weather was like. Boo.

We've spent the last month trekking through Rajasthan, learning way too much about the mating habits of camels and dipping our toes in the nectar (looked like water with goldfish in it to me) of the Golden Temple in the Punjab. Great fun all around!

We made it to the Pakistani border but not into Pakistan because the visa issue seemed like way too much effort and expense. The nightly "Closing of the Border" ceremony was well worth the trip though. Soldiers on both sides strut, march and kick their way to national superiority in a routine of funny walks that would put John Cleese to shame. The crowd was one of the most extreme I've seen so far – with fully grown men pushing grannies to the ground to get a better view of the action. Thankfully our "foreign tourist" status allowed us entry to the VIP section of the bleachers. It was so much fun cheering on India and waving our paper flags like mad.

I'll let you know if we get an audience with His Holiness or if we have to settle for spending our time here eating the first decent western food we've found in months. Either way, I'm glad we're here.

Return of the Lama

Because I know you were waiting with bated breath, here's an update:

We couldn't get security clearance to see the Dalai Lama because they'd reached their foreign visitor quota. Sitting outside a café this morning, we were lamenting how close we'd come to seeing him only to be turned away when a motorcade crept past us, and low and behold! His Holiness was inside peeking out at us from behind his trademark glasses and giving us a wave! Hurrah!

Sure, it's not as good as meeting him but we'll take what we can get. Our karma must have improved just by being in such close proximity to him!

Namaste India

I'm sure you'll all be devastated to hear that this is my last dispatch from India. We've spent the past ten days or so trying to even out our face/hands/feet tan back in Goa, but tomorrow we will begin the arduous thirty-six-hour train/plane/automobile trek to London and then back to Canada.

Thank you all for listening to my ramblings along the way and for the much-needed encouragement when I thought I couldn't take another street molestation or sleeper bus journey. And if you'll bear with me one moment more, I'd also like to thank the following:

the good people of India for their unflagging hospitality (and for speaking English! Hurrah!),

Andy for never once trying to smother me while I slept, even though I surely deserved it on a few occasions,

the dollar-to-rupee exchange rate for taking me so far on so little, and

the lovely people who make antibiotics and the beautiful pharmacists of India who never ask to see a prescription.

Love and kisses,

Kat

TRAVELLING SOLO

Subject: Shiva's Dance
From: Janis Harper

When I'm travelling solo in a country like India, as I did last year, I become hyper-aware – which for me means that I can sometimes see through things to their quantum-physics centres of nothing-but-energy. This can be disconcerting, but is as close as one can get, I think, to "the ultimate reality," the real stuff, without needing to be enlightened. Gone are the comfy, safe structures of home and established routine; gone are familiar faces and neighbourhoods; gone is the known culture, the social dynamics that uphold the values and expectations and etiquette that you've ascribed to, in some degree or other, for most of your life. It really is just you in the big world – and when you travel alone, that's how it is on every level. It's all you.

When I travel by myself, the world ceases to be a solid environment that I can make my way in. Rather, it becomes a malleable dreamscape, constantly shifting and vibrating, reflecting my thoughts and beliefs (whether I'm consciously aware of them at the time or not) and whatever else. The environment is as much in me as I am in it. Boundaries are elusive. Everything is possible. This perspective seems especially appropriate in India, whose ancient spiritual wisdom reveals the physical world and all of its objects, draws and drama as *maya*, illusion, a veil hiding the ultimate reality.

True travellers, those who put themselves out there, alone, vulnerable and open to it all, experience magical things on the road: "coincidences" and "small-world" events occur regularly, and the unexplainable becomes more commonplace. Here's one small example. An Israeli man I met in a Goan guesthouse over a discussion of his book about Jung's archetypes would appear whenever I drew out of my journal a piece of paper that he'd written his email address on. The first time this happened I hadn't seen him for weeks, having been on the road myself and just returned to Goa, and I was wondering if Daniel was still around. I noticed his email address when I was writing in my journal on the beach and decided to head to an internet place to email him. I took a few steps down the beach, and there he was!

The next time it happened I was in Hampi, Karnataka – a different state in South India – and had no idea Daniel would be going there too. I came across his name on that piece of paper while having breakfast in a rooftop restaurant, thought warmly of him, felt an opening in the air around me, walked down the stairs and out into the street, and there he was. He looked different this time, and I didn't recognize him at first: shaved head with a little tail of hair, and dressed all in white, holy Hindu-style. He approached me when I was talking with an Indian man and just stood in front of us for a while, smiling broadly and waiting for me to recognize him.

The last time I saw Daniel, my last day in India before my journey home, we were climbing down the rocky Hemakuta hill in Hampi from where we had just watched the sun set and drunk a small *chai* bought from a little girl, and I heard Daniel softly singing John Denver's song, "Take Me Home, Country Roads." The temple where we were headed cast a long, intricate shadow on our path, the air was warm and smoky, and I was already feeling nostalgic for India. Daniel's choice of song moved me, especially when I realized it was in my honour, and I joined in. That song took us all the way to the temple, where we breathed incense and performed *pujas* in the dark.

When I returned home to Vancouver after seven weeks in India, on my first unsettled day back, I was unpacking my journal and Daniel's piece of paper fell out. Moments later, I opened a cupboard drawer and facing me was a book with the title *Country Roads*, a collection of photos of the Canadian countryside that I'd recently acquired and forgotten I'd stashed in that drawer. Suddenly I was in India again, singing down a darkening hill.

But this kind of story is common among solo travellers. Time is an illusion, a human construct, and synchronicity brings this home in full force. And we take delight in the meaningful "coincidence"; it shakes things up. We are all connected anyway, and on some deep level, we know this. When we travel – when all of the homey structures that we've built around us fall away, and it's just us in the world, alone and shining – the veil of *maya* parts, momentarily providing us glimpses of how it really is.

Daniel would say that there are only two real forces: love and fear. Love is the ultimate reality, and fear is the illusory one and the reason for erecting those structures that keep us "safe," that keep out the bad guys, the bad thoughts, the wrong stuff. Love and Fear. Heaven and Hell. Freedom and Entrapment. The dance between these two forces becomes very visible in India, where a moment of immense connection with another, or being on the receiving end of astounding hospitality or generosity from a poverty-stricken family, can turn into the next moment of being suspicious of getting scammed and afraid of losing belongings, money, passport or even your own life. Love/communion/kindness and fear/anger/suspicion all fall over one another in a rapid acrobatic display, and life becomes a wondrous carnival that one can view from various perspectives. Or, as it's commonly put: you either love or hate India, and usually you do both in the same day.

The solo traveller often becomes aware of the presence of death and how one's own could occur at any moment. This isn't morbid; it's just true. And if you remove the fear from this awareness, as best as you can, life becomes even more real because you're suddenly in the present, fully. Like the magical coincidence and the small-world moments, death-awareness helps us to see the big picture and free ourselves from time.

Learning to live with constant death-awareness is a common spiritual discipline. And in India, any traveller who takes a ride in a bus or taxi becomes very much aware of her imminent death! It's a practical thing that India forces us into, with spiritual side-benefits. We have to learn how to surrender to this possibility, and be calm – otherwise we'd never psychologically survive the white-knuckled strain of the constant sudden swerving into oncoming traffic in the opposite lane, the continual "chicken" games, the break-neck speeds, the blatant disregard of all traffic signals, lights, and order, the speeding up for pedestrians. We'd probably forget to breathe and faint from lack of oxygen.

Most vehicles have a big sign on their rear bumper (beside the one that names the driver's favourite deity, for protection) that says, "HONK please!" I came to understand that honking is a way of saying, "I'm here!" or "I'm here and I'm going to overtake you!" It's a kind of driving etiquette. And there is no break in the cacophonous honking on Indian roads, not for a second.

The ending of a life in India isn't such a tragedy as it is in Canada. Death is everywhere here, integrated into life – from the freshly killed motorcyclist on the highway, covered up with newspapers, that I saw from my bus window ("He is finished!" the man sitting next to me announced gaily, head wagging enthusiastically, as we rode past) to rotting cow and dog carcasses on the ground. There is no real end anyway: only one life, this one, is finished. If you're up for more, you will be reincarnated. In Varanasi, the sacred heart of India, the holy life force of the Ganges River is full of rotting bodies and flaming funeral pyres, absorbing death and offering the same water to the living who immerse themselves in it as a healing blessing, the same water that performs the mundane duty of getting clothes clean. In India, you can witness Shiva's destroyer-creator dance in the dizzying swirl of everyday life. Life and Death and Laundry. In the same sacred river.

And, as Heraclitus said, you can't step in the same river twice. It's a different India I'm in now, a year later, because I'm travelling with my sixteen-year-old son, Adam, this time. Travelling alone and travelling with Adam are vastly different: being with Adam is like carrying a piece of Canada with me, a piece of home. It has a normalizing, comforting effect. It's not me alone in the world, unfettered and undefined, but rather already playing a role in it. I can't see through things so well because I'm trying to see through Adam's eyes. Adam creates a buffer between me and India, in all of her fierce life-death dualities and silky, colour-soaked veils of *maya*. This India is more opaque, though just as teeming and chaotic, and I am a sightseer this time, separate and wonderstruck. I am a mother sharing India with her son; I am no longer dancing with Shiva on the bright edges.

Subject: The Taste of a Tomato
From: Vawn Himmelsbach

Dear Sunita,

I remember when we were kids, dressing up in your *saris* in the basement of your parents' house. I knew your parents had moved from India to northern Alberta long before you were born, that they had an arranged marriage and that you had really cool mirrored elephants around the house. That's about all I knew of India back then – that, and how your dad said, "This is not a tomato," when referring to Canadian tomatoes.

Before I went to India, I didn't quite understand what that meant.

And he didn't understand why I'd want to go to India – for fun. India, after all, isn't exactly a place you go to chill out. If I wanted that, I'd go to Railey Beach in Thailand, or hang out along the Mekong River in Laos where it's easy to lose track of time and forget what day of the week it is.

India, on the other hand, is an assault to the senses: the crowds, the smells, the spiciness of the food, the constant honking of horns. Rickshaw drivers swerve into oncoming traffic and somehow manage to avoid cars, pedestrians and holy cows. Child beggars with snotty noses and pleading eyes pull at your sleeve, asking for money. That tasty mango lassi leaves you with a severe case of Delhi Belly and a late-night date with the toilet in your hotel room. So, really, your dad has a point. Why on earth did I come to this godforsaken country?

There are a lot of reasons that sound good, in theory. There are some pretty impressive sights: the Taj Mahal, of course, and plenty of forts, palaces and ancient ruins. There are gurus and holy men and ashrams for those who seek enlightenment. There are beaches and cheap beer and parties in Goa for those who seek a good time. There are camels in the Rajasthani desert and Bollywood starlets in Mumbai and British hill stations in the Indian Himalayas.

But then there are all those things you can't plan for. The things you don't read about in glossy travel brochures. Like the heat. Your carefully planned itinerary – the one that seemed to make sense while flipping through your *India Lonely Planet* at a Second Cup café while a snowstorm raged outside – is no match for the heat. It takes over, suffocates your energy, destroys your best intentions. You only want to lie in your hotel room, underneath the ceiling fan, with a wet sarong wrapped around you, trying to cool off.

The bus schedule doesn't make sense. The rickshaw drivers don't take you where you want to go. You somehow find yourself sitting in a government emporium with men rolling out expensive carpets at your feet. But then, the unexpected happens. Once I heard monks chanting while sitting in a rose garden. Another time, I was taken aback when I tasted the best *chai* I've ever had – out of a disposable ceramic cup at a dingy-looking street stall. I think I paid about two cents for it. And another time, two young men asked me if they could take a photo of me with their lovely, charming grandmother.

One minute you're on a high, soaking it all up, living in the moment. The next you're in the depths of despair, wishing you were anywhere but India. Often, several times in a day.

I had a night like that. It was one of those nights where I experienced the best and the worst of India, all in a twelve-hour time span. It started off, as so many stories do, with a boy. But this is no love story.

⌒

India has a bit of a reputation among foreign women. If you're travelling solo, "accidental" touching, purposeful groping and lewd comments are, sadly, par for the course.

I was in Rishikesh during a festival – a festival that only occurs once every decade, which meant thousands upon thousands of Hindu pilgrims had descended upon what is supposedly a quiet, laid-back town known for its ashrams. It also meant I had a hell of a time getting a bus ticket back to Delhi, so I was stuck with the night bus. Supposedly it was a "deluxe" bus with reclining seats and air conditioning. But I've spent enough time in Asia to know I'd probably be spending the night in a death-trap-on-wheels with Bollywood music blaring out of the speakers all night long.

When I arrived at the bus station, it was late, it was dark, and I couldn't see any other foreigners around. And my ticket didn't seem to match the number of any buses in the compound. A young man approached, showed me an official-looking badge and addressed me in English. He explained that he was with the tourist commission, and his job was to help foreigners like me get on the right bus. Naturally, I was skeptical – as you are when travelling alone as a woman in a foreign country. But, true to his word, he led me to a bus that was, at the very least, heading to Delhi, though it was far from "deluxe."

The young man told me that the only seat left was at the back of the bus. I wasn't thrilled. The last row is, by far, the worst place to sit because you can't recline your seat, and you feel every bump in the road – not ideal for an overnight bus trip when you want to at least attempt to sleep. When I sat down, the young man started lecturing me on how I should watch my bag and keep my wits about me. I tuned out. I had heard it all before; I knew the drill. But I smiled politely as he yammered on.

Then, the unexpected happened – or perhaps I should say "expected." He asked me if I had a boyfriend. I lied, of course. I said he was waiting for me in Delhi. I invented a name, an occupation, even a story of how we had first met. Not that it mattered. He leaned in and kissed me on the cheek. I was startled, but not frightened. After all, I think he weighed about eighty pounds – I could have beaten him to a pulp if I had wanted to. I was just annoyed. I reprimanded him; he looked ashamed, apologized and left. For a few minutes, anyway.

The young man returned to tell me that God must have willed it that I be with a better man than him. Then, as if proving his unworthiness, he moved in for a grope. He was quick, but not quick enough. Fortunately, my years of training in martial arts has engrained in me an automatic response to attack – or, in this case, grope. He left empty-handed, so to speak. I rolled my eyes in disgust. This was one of those moments when I hated India.

I tried to find another seat closer to the front of the bus next to a woman – to no avail. That's when another young man spoke up, in English, and offered me the seat next to him.

When you're travelling alone, you learn to fine-tune your intuition and trust your instincts. At home, we function on autopilot so much of the time, or rely on the advice of friends and family, that we're often completely out of touch with our intuitive nature. Travel heightens our awareness, sharpens our senses, so it becomes part of the way we function. And in India, it's essential.

When I first met the young man who claimed to be with the tourist commission (and probably actually was), I had an uneasy feeling. I felt uncomfortable sitting at the back of the bus, in the dark, literally backed into a corner. This time, however, my gut was telling me that it was okay to sit next to this man. Sometimes, too, you just have to trust people. It's easy to become paranoid when you're travelling solo, like everyone is out to screw you over, but the reality is far more people have gone out of their way to help me than hurt me.

So I sat down, reluctantly. His cell phone rang. He chatted away to someone in Hindi. He hung up. He told me he was a musician on his way to Mumbai. A singer. That he was travelling with his band. Right. He asked me about Canada. His cell rang again. After a few minutes, he turned to me and said his girlfriend was on the phone and wanted to practice her English with me. If his intention was to disarm me, it worked.

At this point, the entire bus was focused on our conversation, whispering, giggling, making comments I couldn't understand. All of a sudden, the young man stood up and lectured everyone in rapid Hindi – to a round of cheers and applause. When he sat down, he told me what he had said: that I was a guest to this country, and he wanted me to have fond memories of my time here.

I didn't sleep that night – and it wasn't because my seat barely reclined and there was no air conditioning, or I felt I was leaving my life in the hands of a wild-eyed bus driver. I stayed up chatting to the musician, comparing our very different lives. Sure enough, his band was actually on the bus with their wives and babies, and they came over, bringing us home-cooked food that we ate with our right hand – some of the best food I've had in India. At a rest stop in the middle of the night, we stretched our legs under the starry sky, surrounded by eucalyptus trees, drinking hot *chai*. At one point, I ended up holding someone's baby. By the time we arrived in Delhi at about 6:00 AM, I was in love with India again.

And so it goes. I have a love-hate relationship with India. It's not an easy place for outsiders, especially if you're an unmarried woman travelling alone. It can be exhausting – physically, emotionally. So why is it that I've been to India twice and plan to return again next year? Why can't I just be content to hang out at a resort in Cancun?

I've given this a lot of thought, especially in those moments when I desperately want to get on a plane and fly back to the "normalcy" of Canada. Maybe it's because India is the anti-Cancun. It's not about turning your brain off and numbing the stress of an office job in buffets and booze. In India, you're forced to pay attention, to be aware, to live in the moment. You see sides of yourself that you didn't know existed, good and bad. It pushes you to your limits, and sometimes your reactions surprise you. But that should come as no surprise. India is full of unexpected twists and turns, whether it's a bus trip or a journey inward.

So I get why some people don't understand the allure of India. I get why your dad thinks I'm crazy for travelling to India. But *if I never went there* then I wouldn't know what a tomato is actually supposed to taste like. And I wouldn't know that I'm strong enough to deal with groping boys. And, perhaps most importantly, I wouldn't have met the musician and his band on a bus headed to Mumbai – my fondest memory of India, one that far surpasses seeing the Taj Mahal.

Your oldest friend,

Vawn

DELHI

Subject: Getting Settled
From: Margaret Miller

Dear Auntie Margaret,

Shortly after I talked to you on the phone from the airport, I was on the plane and headed for Delhi. Perhaps not surprisingly, it was a long and gruelling flight that was late in arriving. But my dear hotel proprietor, Prem, was waiting in the crowd gathered at Arrivals, holding up a sign with my name on it. He drove me to the hotel in Vasant Kunj, arriving at 2:30 AM; I woke up at 8:00 AM and was propelled straight away into Delhi time.

My first day began with Prem inviting me to ride with him while he ran his errands. I saw something of the centre of the city, with Prem providing a running commentary, pointing out the Delhi Ridge, the Presidential Palace, India Gate, Embassy Row. The people from the countryside who came to build the American Embassy School are now living in a previously vacant space across the street, sleeping under tarpaulins and eating and cleaning outside. The traffic is intense, and they are building more and more roads, but Prem tells me (and it is apparent) that the city is also constructing a massive metro system which, when completed, will drastically reduce traffic congestion, or so it is hoped. Yet you have to wonder, as this city is evidently in love with the automobile. When I stepped off the plane, my senses were assaulted by the smell of car exhaust, and I could feel my sinuses become increasingly more scratchy and annoyed as the days passed.

Prem himself is a proud and happy member of a three-car family – one for himself, one for his wife and one for his sister-in-law. In the course of our drive I learned that the hotel is only one of their family businesses. They also own a factory which manufactures clothing for overseas clients and a business which deconstructs used overseas oil refineries and transports them to India where they are reconstructed and resold. In addition to his wife and sister-in-law, he lives with his two children and an extremely friendly and persistent daschund named Tuffie. I met the children and Tuffie during our day's travels when we picked the children up from school and dropped them off at their tutors (evidently a common practice for well-off Indians, who want their children to have a head start in a very competitive educational system).

Prem, I also learned, had a remarkable story to tell. He was working in the U.S. in 2001 and had a reserved seat on one of the planes that, on September 11th, flew into one of the World Trade Center buildings. On September 9th, a woman colleague called and asked him if he would like her to change his reservation to the 10th; she was flying that day and thought it would be nice if they travelled together. He agreed, and so it was that he was on the ground in Washington DC the next day. Needless to say, Prem considered himself to be a very lucky man.

Before returning to the hotel, we drove to Paharganj, a chaotically crowded backpackers' enclave close to the main train station. We were there to pick up Ellen, a young Norwegian woman. Ellen was struggling with the fact that in India her brilliant blonde hair brought her much unwanted male attention. I gather that in Paharganj she had found this attention to be particularly intense and so made arrangements to move to Prem's hotel. Ellen was profoundly deaf and, as I don't know sign language, we communicated with a combination of writing and hand gestures. She had just come from Nepal where she had had a glorious time, including her first experience of hang gliding. It was amazing, she said – utterly liberating. She taught me how to say "*Om*" in Nepalese sign language.

I think I told you that one of the first things I wanted to do when I got here was to go to the National Museum, so the following morning Prem walked me down to the main road and waited with me until the bus arrived. The bus, which was a screeching and barrelling adventure in itself, cost ten rupees and had designated seats for women. Between two of the stops a tiny, very dark, young woman wearing a bright pink *sari* and holding a baby got on the bus. As we flew down the road she walked dramatically up and down the aisle, singing her song in a beautifully high voice. Just before the stop, she stopped singing, collected a few coins from the passengers and stepped down to the pavement.

I spent several (increasingly jet-lagged) hours at the museum, admiring in particular the ancient stone sculptures of voluptuous goddesses; stunning bronzes of Shiva, Lord of the Dance; and exquisite miniature paintings created by the artists of the Mughal court. On my way home I purchased two coconuts from a street vendor – my first (inept) bargaining experience. That evening I shared them with Ellen over our meal of *daal* and *roti* in the hotel dining room. They had a lovely smooth and fleshy texture that reminded me of crab meat.

Yesterday morning I packed up my bag, found an auto-rickshaw (actually, yes, it was Prem who found it for me) and headed off through the Delhi rush-hour traffic to my new office in Hauz Khas. Smriti, the intern coordinator, met me and outlined something of what I will be doing over the next three months. My first project will be to work with a local teacher to develop a curriculum around food issues for school children. In the last ten years, there has been a spike in childhood obesity in India due to the influx of western-style fast food and eating habits. This curriculum will therefore address issues of false health/nutrition claims, the impact of junk food on the land and water supply, and food politics. The teacher is also keen to address the representation of girls in fast food ads and the pressures felt by young Indian girls to conform to a western ideal of beauty.

Smriti then took me to my flat, which is a five-minute walk from the office. We walked by dozens of sleeping dogs that she told me to be wary of, especially at night when they form into packs. At the moment, I will be the only person living in the flat, although I should have company soon. It is a huge apartment – I judge it to be about 1,200 square feet – and is beautifully decorated with tribal hangings, lovely tiled floors and, in the kitchen, a garlanded picture of Krishna. However, the bathroom has its challenges. The shower head has five streams of water, each of which strikes off in its own direction; as there is no shower curtain, it gets quite exciting in the bathroom during shower time. But, strangely, it works.

This morning, before beginning the day, I sat in the kitchen listening to the sounds of my new neighbourhood. There is little car traffic in the early morning, and other sounds come to the surface. This morning I could hear the men calling as they pushed their carts of vegetables and fruit down the coming-to-life streets. Others ride by on bicycles, carrying bags of scavenged paper and calling, "Oh-ay-YAH!"

More, another day.

Love, your niece,

Margaret

Subject: Festival of Lights

From: Liz Snell

For the past week or so, piles of tiny clay lanterns and stores hung with strings of flowered, flashing lights have lined New Delhi's market streets. Everywhere are tables of vibrant-coloured little gods: monkey-faced Hanuman, the elephant-god Ganesh and blue-skinned Krishna. Men squat on wooden carts and thread together long strings of marigolds and folded ashok leaves to hang from doorways. Stands appear, filled with sticky round balls of puffed corn and rice, rough white shapes of elephants that look like moulded wax but are actually pure sugar, and huge bags of popcorn. I've bought six little clay lanterns shaped like leaves, peacocks, paisleys, and hands holding a lotus flower, all brushed with gold around the rims, ready to be filled with wick and oil. The air is electric, and the boys on our street have exploded firecrackers on our street for days.

Today, Diwali is finally here. It's the biggest Hindu festival of the year and symbolically lights the way home for Rama with his rescued bride, Sita. It also welcomes the goddess of wealth, Lakshmi, to the new Hindu financial year. With its sweets and fireworks, it feels a bit like Halloween, which falls at almost the same time. But I squint at the strings of lights draped on the houses and try to imagine it's an early Christmas.

When it's dark out, I go down to the street to see what my neighbourhood is up to. The gang of boys on our street is, predictably, setting off firecrackers. Since the last firecracker-festival, Dussehra, I've determined to make friends with our neighbours as best I can.

Since I see the boys most often, I always say hello to them and try to win them over. They all speak very good English so it's easy to talk to them. The two I see most often are a sleepy-eyed boy with rectangular glasses and his tall, gangly friend. Tonight I take pictures of their houses, and they all clamour to pose in front of the lights. When I wave goodbye to the boys, one of them still jumps up and down in hysteric excitement over the photos.

At the end of our street, I turn left and walk down towards the market. I snap shots of little girls in western clothes who sell lanterns, of a bicycle piled with boxes of incense for sale, and of a man who sells all kinds of inflated balloons that glow like glass in the light from the shops.

The best shop on this street is the sweet shop. It's a long, narrow store with one table that runs its entire length. On the table are large open containers filled with sweets that you can scoop into boxes: fibrey squares of *soan papdi* studded with pistachios, grainy yellow balls of *ladoo*, chocolate-covered squares of shortbread-like *barfi* coated in silver foil and many more. As a child in Canada, I liked the greasy, crisp orange curls of *jalebi*, but my new favourite sweet is *gulab jamun*, little brown balls rather like Timbits soaked in syrup. I decide to buy a box for the boys on our street and push my way into the crowded shop, past men in blue sarongs who carry trays of sweets out the door above their heads. I lean over the counter, crushed on every side.

"Do you need help?" On my right, a girl a bit younger than me addresses me in perfect English.

"Thanks for asking," I say, surprised. "I just want a mix of sweets for the boys on my street."

"Are you here alone?" she asks.

"No, I live with my friend."

"I mean, are you alone at the market tonight?"

I notice she's accompanied by an elderly man in a white turban, probably her father.

"Oh, yes I am," I reply.

"No offence, but it's not really a good time to come here."

I laugh. "I always come at the wrong time – it's okay."

She looks at me solemnly. "No, what I mean is, it's not really safe."

I shrug my shoulders and thank her for her help. I can feel the man behind me pressing against me, and although it's so crowded he probably has no choice, I clutch my box of *gulab jamun* and turn to work my way out of the tight mass. If I were a good Indian girl, I'm sure I'd worry far more than I do. But Diwali will only come once while I'm here, so I have to make the most of it.

As I walk back down the street, I eat a few of the *gulab jamun* and stop to buy apples and bananas from one of the fruit carts. The sleepy-eyed boy is the first one I see. I hand him the box and say, "Share them with your friends. Happy Diwali."

When he pulls off the top of the box, all his friends crowd around. "Happy Diwali," they all call after me. "Come back for fireworks at ten."

As I walk back to my apartment, I see them point at me as they share the sweets with an old woman.

At 10:00 PM, I slip on my Indian leather shoes, grab my camera and head down to the smoky street. Besides all the electric lights, little clay lamps now line all the verandas and walls. Fireworks shred the street into ribbons and fractions of sound and light. I hide behind the cars, where I wince at the loudest crackers and stare open-mouthed at the swoosh of sparkles that split the dark. I nod at all the neighbours: the little girl who holds a sparkler beside a group of women on the veranda (where good girls belong, not in the market), a girl my age dressed in a fancy sleeveless *kameez*, ready for a party, and the guard who wears round glasses and smiles at me whenever I walk past the little booth he sits outside.

In a plastic chair a few doors down from ours sits a large Sikh man with a white beard and an orange turban. I've seen him often, and I smile as I near him. He extends his hand towards me and motions to his house. At the gate, his wife stands and beckons me. Why does she want to invite me in? I don't think we've ever met before. She takes my hand, and I follow her inside.

"Come, come in, sit down." She pulls up a plastic chair for me and hands me a cup of *chai*. "This is my daughter, Priti."

Priti wears western clothes and is about my age. She soon disappears into the back room, where she calls out answers to her mother's questions every now and then. The room we're in is small, crammed with a table and three beds, as is common in India. On the opposite wall, I notice a picture of two hands, palms out, with lines and letters diagrammed across them.

Inder, as she's called, is a large woman, her round face slightly pock-marked and her forehead yellow with turmeric paste. She speaks good English, and I soon learn she practices homeopathic medicine in her home. She gets me to stand on a machine that looks like it's from the 1950s: a green metal box surmounted by two black pressure-point massage pads for the feet. When she turns it on, she holds my sweaty hand and says, "You won't fall off, don't worry."

I can't stop laughing – it tickles. Proudly, she points out her other two "machines," one for spinal problems, the other for migraines and other head problems. I wonder how she decided to go into homeopathy, so I ask, "Why do you do this?"

"It's my career, just like teaching is yours," she explains. "I want to help people, to better the world."

I grimace. "Well, you're probably bettering the world more than my teaching is."

"I was a teacher too," she says. "Then I got married and my in-laws wanted me to stay at home, so I switched occupations."

But she doesn't stay at home; she rides her scooter every day to Mayfair Garden, where her business has a "nanotechnology" machine that can tell you "everything wrong with your body."

"Your family is in Canada?" she asks.

"Yes."

"Will they come here?"

"I don't know."

"If they come, bring them to meet me. I love meeting people; it's my hobby. I like people with all different views and beliefs."

I lean towards her. "Me too!"

I'm surprised to find someone like this here. She listens to me like I really matter, even though I can't speak Hindi, and it's just what I need.

"I feel homesick. I miss home today," I say.

She smiles at me. "Well, just come to me and you won't miss home!"

One of the dusty, nicked-up dogs that lives on our street noses around Inder's ankles. She slaps him lovingly on the side. "This is Babu. He was a street dog, but now he's my dog. He knows Hindi: when I tell him to sit, he sits; when I tell him to stay, he stays."

"What does 'Babu' mean?"

"Cutie – like 'you're so cute,'" Inder replies as I let Babu sniff my hand. "So when will you come to Mayfair Garden with me to see my machine?"

What is this "machine," I wonder. I take Inder's number and tell her I'll call her. We grasp each other's hand goodbye. "Very nice to meet you!" I smile again at her husband, who's still outside in his chair.

When I get home, my roommate Sarah smiles. "Your bedroom's nice and smoky."

It's true – I left my windows open and now a smoky haze blurs the air. Before I climb into bed, I take my six little clay lanterns and prop them up along the ledge of the window above the door. The sound of late-night Diwali firecrackers sings me to sleep.

Subject: Old Delhi, New Tricks

From: Farah Ghuznavi

Let me say at the outset that this message comes to you courtesy of one-and-a-half cheese *masala dosas* and the most enormous vanilla-enriched cold coffee milkshake I've ever consumed – that too, at 9:00 PM in a country that doesn't quite see the point of decaf! But after the day that Katy and I have just survived, I will confess to savouring every miniscule caffeinated jolt of that delicious concoction. I never thought I'd say this, but who needs beer when you can have a milkshake like this at the end of a long, hot day of "doing India"?

I can just imagine the look of horror on your face as you read that beer comment . . . . Don't worry, there's some distance to travel before I turn teetotal, but I fear that this trip *is* changing me in mysterious ways. For example, while vegetarianism has never really appealed to me, I am now perilously near to being seduced into the belief that this could be a viable lifestyle.

Part of this vegetarian wanna-be(haviour) on my part can, of course, be attributed to the amazing variety of non-sentient – or more accurately, "never-were-sentient" – items that make up the gastronomic final frontier in the Indian restaurants the two of us have been exploring. Furthermore, after today's experience, I'm convinced that *dosas* must be the ultimate comfort food, specially designed for the spicily-inclined. I mean, how can you go wrong with a deceptively feather-light wrapping of paper-thin savoury pastry deep-fried and filled with deliciously seasoned potatoes, with a little chopped carrot and a few peas thrown in as a nod to healthy eating? The generous amount of cheese lining the inside of my *dosa* really put the comfort into this bout of comfort eating.

The day started well, since Katy and I were both determined to get in as much activity as possible before the melting caramel haze of the intense afternoon heat seeped into our bones and sapped our determination to make the most of this two-week break in northern India. We should have known better, I suppose, than to arrive in Delhi at what is still the height of summer – though the autumnal shades of early September in London had lulled us both into believing that India would just be a warmer version of what we were so keen to leave behind.

Although I was born across India's far away eastern border, in Bangladesh, the many intervening years spent studying and working in Britain have left me completely disoriented in terms of how the subcontinent functions, from its weather patterns to the vagaries of public transport and the eccentric characters one invariably encounters in the course of travelling. And while that wouldn't be considered an acceptable excuse by any of my South Asian brethren, the truth is I have more than once on this trip found myself experiencing the peculiar disorientation of a brown foreigner.

My Hindi – which is the closest that northern India comes to having a lingua franca – is a lot worse than rusty; it's more like fossilized, based as it is almost entirely on a childhood diet of occasional Bollywood movies and a few family vacations. Needless to say, on the latter occasions, I at least had the luxury of relying on my parents, who both grew up under the British Raj and are fluent in Hindi. Unlike them, my Hindi is in such appalling shape that an Indian friend in London had warned Katy that she mustn't rely on my non-existent communication skills. "I don't know what language Farah's speaking, but it's certainly not Hindi!" she'd said, laughingly dismissing my halting attempts to articulate a few basic sentences.

In some ways, this trip has been a lot simpler for Katy – as a white Englishwoman who speaks only her mother tongue, she has nothing to prove; she can, without embarrassment, explain away almost any faux pas on her legitimately alien status. Luckily, most of the Indians we've interacted with to date have spoken enough English to render my unintelligible linguistic efforts pretty much redundant. That is, until today.

We'd spent the morning visiting old Delhi, especially the area around the Red Fort. The architecture dates back to the Mughal period of Muslim rule in northern India, and the building style is a wonderful melange of arched entranceways; spacious apartments reaching up to touch soaring, domed ceilings; and manicured gardens full of colourful blossoms and verdant plant life, complemented by the luminous blades of emerald-green grass that spring forth from every inch of ground.

As usual, we came across a group of young men who wanted to practice their English language skills on us. Fed up of negotiating this particular gauntlet, an inspired Katy decided to deny her heritage in order to avoid the stilted conversation that was likely to follow. In response to "Where are you from, sister?" she replied without batting an eyelid, "Norway." The conversation that followed did not quite go according to script. In amazement, a couple of the boys cried out, "Nowhere? How can you be from nowhere?" So I stepped in and said, "She doesn't speak much English. She is from Norway. You know, N-O-R-W-A-Y?"

"Oh yes, we know Norway," one of the boys responded gamely. He proceeded to respond in kind, "And we are from India, I-N-D-I-A!" They were good sports, so we humoured their request and ended up taking one of the group photos that is so close to the South Asian heart before moving on.

Dipping into some of the souvenir shops near the entrance of the Red Fort, we emerged with small treasures: sets of beautifully-made glass animals in swirling shades of red, green, blue, yellow and black, ranging from the more familiar standard dimensions to the fingernail-sized versions, rendered to perfection in each instance; intricately embroidered cloth wallets and purses; carved wooden miniature chess sets; jewel-coloured patterns of flowers and geometric shapes inlaid into white marble boxes of various shapes and sizes, reminiscent of the Taj Mahal marble work; and Katy's favourite, small red seeds that had been hollowed out and filled with fragments of bone, miraculously carved into tiny animal shapes, clearly visible only through a magnifying glass.

After a respectable afternoon siesta, we re-emerged from our hotel room to venture into the crowded alleyways of Delhi West in search of the famous restaurant, Karim's. This has always been a Ghuznavi family favourite, though I haven't been there in almost twenty years. In the end, I managed to locate the restaurant, and we laid to rest (or so I thought at the time) the possibility of a vegetarian lifestyle once and for all.

What followed was an orgy of grilled meats, kebabs on a skewer and, so that Katy could prove her "adventure traveller" credentials, a surprisingly delicious dish of sheep's brain *masala*, helped down by a selection of *rotis*, breads of various types and textures. A minor detour for the mandatory *paan* followed; this betel leaf and chopped betel nut confection is garnished with a white paste that's notorious for providing a narcotic kick to the senses. It's highly addictive, and side-effects include a tendency to produce copious quantities of scarlet spit.

We decided to work off some of the gluttonous calories we'd absorbed by taking a brief tour around the nearby shrine of Nizamuddin, which is the mausoleum of the Sufi saint, Nizamuddin Auliya. The Sufis belong to a Muslim sect that takes a distinctly "peace and love" approach to all religions and humanity as a whole, emphasizing spirituality and co-existence. The place attracts people of all faiths and has a wonderful atmosphere of calm despite the crowds that make their way there to worship. This shrine also featured in the highly controversial Indo-Canadian film *Fire* where the female protagonists found refuge after escaping domestic violence. We passed a couple of peaceful hours just people-watching and drinking in the atmosphere there before making our way back to the main road.

I would like to blame what happened next on the narcotic in the *paan*, but that wouldn't be fair since we'd both spat out the mangled green concoction into the nearest rubbish bin. I had once again let down my origins by doing so with an unbecoming speed, even faster than Katy managed to get rid of hers. But I think that the sinful indulgence of that meat-heavy meal may have had something to do with lulling us into a stupor of sorts. Or maybe we were just blissed-out by our time at the shrine. Anyway, we climbed into one of the three-wheeled motorized scooters that litter the streets of the capital, and I instructed the driver to take us back to our hotel in Jorbagh.

It was only after we'd been riding for some time that I began to get nervous about where we were heading. It seemed to be taking a lot longer to get back than it had on the way out. A couple of times, I reminded the driver that we wanted to go to Jorbagh. He nodded his head rhythmically back and forth in that uniquely Indian way that was presumably meant to be reassuring. But when we began once again driving away from the centre of the city into what looked like its outskirts, I could not dismiss my increasing sense of anxiety.

We didn't have to wait much longer for enlightenment. Drawing the scooter to a screeching halt on the side of a dusty road in the midst of decidedly unfamiliar surroundings, the driver indicated that we had arrived. The question was, where? The place appeared to be some kind of industrial suburb, with no sign of any tourist accommodation in sight. Upon inquiry, the driver informed us that we were now in Karolbagh (which he pronounced to rhyme with our original destination, Jorbagh, as "Krorebagh"). If we now wanted to go to Jorbagh – which we should have told him in the first place, he asserted – it would cost us an extra hundred rupees!

I was outraged. It was the most obvious form of extortion. Clearly he had taken us both for idiotic foreigners who had no idea where they were; and the fact that he was partially right didn't make it any easier to swallow. Passers-by began to stare at us with somewhat aggressive curiosity, since it was perfectly clear that we didn't belong there. With twilight descending rapidly, and no other scooters or taxis to be seen, I didn't give much for our chances of finding our way home alone.

Katy stood by the roadside, looking paler and more foreign by the minute, urging me to pay the man whatever he wanted to take us back to Jorbagh. But I'd had enough of being the brown alien. In my appallingly fractured Hindi, I began arguing with him instead. It went on for several minutes; and it felt like a lot longer. To be honest,

I'm not sure what I actually said to him, but perhaps my tone said it all – *his* certainly spoke volumes! In the end, he agreed to take us back for a mere twenty rupees extra. Hiding my relief, I scrambled back into the scooter with poor Katy, who was badly shaken, deprived of even the limited relief of an adrenaline surge born out of righteous indignation.

In less than twenty minutes, we were back in the blessedly familiar environs of Jorbagh. Our scooter driver drove off in a huff, hurling a few choice swear words in my direction as he went. He had understandably expected a better return on his scam than a mere twenty rupees. But I couldn't have cared less. We were home safe – and, surprisingly, the alternating surges of anger and terror (in my case) and sheer terror (in Katy's case) had left us ferociously hungry once again.

Heading for our favourite vegetarian restaurant in nearby Khan Market seemed an apt way to celebrate our deliverance. And the cherry to top off the whipped cream on my delicious drink came in the form of Katy's comment, uttered with unmistakably heartfelt sincerity: "I don't care what *anyone* says about your Hindi – that scooter driver certainly understood what you were saying!"

So it all ended well: we survived our traveller's rite of passage and have already started laughing about it. And on that happy note, I will leave you for this evening. The last bit of my *masala dosa* awaits my attention, and I'm contemplating dessert . . . .

Subject: Without a Face
From: Liz Snell

"She says she loves him already, and she's never even met him."

My American friend, Leslie, refers to Kushboo, my Muslim friend who'll be married tomorrow.

Tonight, nineteen-year-old Kushboo sits on a bed in her living room in Nizamuddin, New Delhi, while her sister-in-law scrawls *mehendi* on all sides of Kushboo's hands and arms, up to her elbows. Dark flowers blossom and spread while her sister-in-law dabs the drying henna with lemon juice to make it darker. When our little group of Canadian and American friends enters the room, Kushboo extends her one undecorated arm to take my hand in hers and welcomes us with quiet, shining eyes. Her hand is faintly yellow. For a few days now, my young friend, Nicole, says, women have rubbed turmeric paste on Kushboo's legs and arms to "make her body smell sweet and give her skin a nice glow." As we sit on the floor, backs to the wall, one of Kushboo's female relatives comes around with a bowl of turmeric paste and smears a wide strip down each of our arms. It smells like lemon. I rub it into my skin and it begins to dry and crumble off.

I stand over Kushboo and watch the *mehendi* continue on the other arm. She motions with one hand to the other. "The groom's name is in here." In between the Indian flowers, there are English letters which spell out his name. Kushboo traces them lightly with her finger. She's delicate and quiet, but with a certain deep strength of peace and character to her, like a small animal that watches everything from the shadows.

Kushboo, whose name means "sweet smell," was sixteen when her mother died. By that point, her father was already gone. Her older brother, Mehaboob, arranged her wedding for her. The match was originally supposed to be for Rehmat or Azmat, Kushboo's older sisters, but since Kushboo is younger and prettier she won out. A girl's hopes here hang entirely on her genes – in the matrimonials, which are pages of personals put out by parents or matchmakers, almost the only requirement for a bride is that she be "beautiful, fair [light-skinned], slim" and sometimes tall or of Brahmin caste. After Kushboo is married, she'll wear a full black *burqa* over her clothes and cook for everyone in her new family – whom she's never met. She's never even seen a picture of her husband-to-be, though he's seen one of her.

I shake my head. "The idea of a western marriage is hard enough for me to swallow, but to leave my life for someone I've never even met . . . . She must be so scared."

Because she doesn't have a mother, she didn't know anything about sex until her sister-in-law, Heena – who has a white, even smile and high cheekbones and kisses her wide-eyed baby on the head – had "The Talk" with her recently.

"She didn't know anything except what she's seen in movies, and you know Bollywood," Leslie says. In Indian movies, even a kiss is very rare, let alone sex scenes. A long embrace or a suggestive dance move is the most they'll show.

We eat Danishes from a bakery in Delhi and a spicy Indian *namkeen* (savoury snack). After sweet, milky *chai*, we decide to leave. Kushboo's sister-in-law hasn't even started *mehendi* on Kushboo's feet, but we need to get some sleep before the wedding.

"See you tomorrow," I say as I slide my shoes on by the door. I glance at Kushboo where she sits in her simple yellow floral *salwar kameez*, surrounded by the family she's grown up with. Her life has reached its turning point. From here on in, everything will change.

꩜

I wish I didn't have to wear my *dupatta* (scarf); it gets in the way and slips up to hide my necklace. I wish I didn't have to wear my pretty sandals either; the rhinestone circles dig into my toes as my American friend, Amy, and I walk to Nicole's house in Nizamuddin.

It took days in the hot, sweaty market to find our outfits. Mine is black and gold, embroidered with tiny beads and mirrors. I feel like a princess from *The Arabian Nights*. In Nicole's house, women come and go from her brother's bedroom. Inside, they deck out Kushboo. Someone asks for perfume, so Amy and I trot back to her place to find some.

When we go inside to give it to Kushboo, I'm stunned. Nicole already showed us Kushboo's *lehenga* before Kushboo had even seen it. We felt the weight of the red skirt and top and marvelled at the intricate embroidery and beading in red, silver and gold. But the figure who stands before us can't be the same girl we saw only the night before.

She stands silently in the middle of the room, barely blinking, with just the slightest smile as we pull out our cameras. Her arms are covered in red and gold bangles, and an elaborate, multi-coloured necklace of gold and pearls sits below her throat, with earrings to match. Her eyelids are painted with thick black kohl and sparkly rose-red shadow; her lips are deep red and outlined even darker. Although Kushboo is no taller than my shoulder, I'm a bit in awe of her in this state.

Azmat, Rehmat and the other women mill about her like courtiers. They drape the glittering *dupatta* over her head, dab perfume behind her ears and finally move her into the living room so she can be properly photographed. She hardly says a word, just looks down demurely and motions every once in a while for someone to get in the photo with her.

Mehaboob appears in a long, embroidered cream silk jacket and pants, complete with a red and gold scarf. He's a tall, handsome man and speaks good English. Nicole's dad, Matt, hugs him like he's his brother.

Matt tells us it's time to leave for the Nizamuddin community centre where the wedding will be held. The women cover Kushboo's face with a lacy black veil and lead her down to the car. The community centre is only a few minutes away by foot, so most of us walk. As usual, only a few stars are visible above, but our glittering parade makes up for the missing constellations. All the walls inside the centre and the high fence and entrance outside are draped in long pieces of sparkly blue, yellow and orange cloth that billow in the breeze.

While the women take Kushboo behind a curtained section to the left of the low stage, I admire all the clothing of the arriving guests. A small group of women are dressed in red *lehengas* as fancy as Kushboo's. "Those are the women who've been married in the last year," Nicole explains. Apparently, wedding clothes are reusable here.

Rehmat often comes alongside me and puts her hand on my arm to explain or ask something in broken English. "Kushboo has a shy nature," she says.

I smile at her. "But she seems very sweet, very lovely."

"Yes, she's a very sweet, simple girl."

Kushboo's sisters are beautiful; they have the same soft eyes and high Indian cheekbones. But their age shows; their skin isn't smooth like Kushboo's, and one has a chipped tooth while the other has a large mole on one side of her nose. They're lovely, gentle women who'd easily marry if matches weren't made solely on looks and age. But I catch no expression of jealousy in either of them. They both seem very happy for Kushboo.

But is Kushboo happy? We go behind the curtain to see how she's doing. She still says nothing as women laugh and press her hands, only looks down at her gold clutch that she holds limply.

Amy leans her head towards me and says softly, "Do you think she's thinking, 'I wonder if he's cute'?"

"I would be," I say. Mehaboob is a good man; he's very gentle towards Kushboo, so I hope he's chosen her match well.

There's a sudden flurry of excitement around the doors. A black car decorated with flowers pulls up outside the entrance. I stand on my toes to get a good look at the groom. Mehaboob and some other men dressed in Muslim white escort him up the walk while cameras flash like it's a red carpet instead of a green one. He's dressed in cream silk and wears a dress turban and a garland of red and white flowers.

"How old do you think he is?" Amy mutters to me.

"I don't know." I'm crestfallen.

I first heard he was twenty-seven, but this man is nowhere near so young. His face has none of the definition of a man in his twenties; his skin is rough and his cheeks are scored with age. We're told he's thirty-one, but Michelle disagrees. "He has to be at least forty."

I try to convince myself he's good-looking; certainly, he could be worse. Looks aren't everything, but since it's an arranged marriage, it's all I have to go on for now.

"As long as Kushboo's happy," Nicole says, then shudders. "But the idea of them together just isn't working for me!"

I don't know whom I have more sympathy for – Kushboo, behind the curtain, or the groom, who constantly wipes his face with a folded square of white cloth and never smiles once.

"He's shy," someone whispers.

The men lead him up onto the stage and sit down in a white-clad group. I go back to visit Kushboo. It's time to insert Kushboo's nose ring. It's as wide as a bangle and decorated with white and red beads. Her nose was only pierced in the last few months, and though she's stretched the hole in preparation for this moment, the stud won't come out. There's a slight air of panic as Heena struggles to loosen it. Finally, someone uses a piece of thread to work it out, and the big hoop completes the ensemble.

Nicole crouches near Kushboo then comes to stand beside me. "Look at her hands – she's shaking, she's so nervous! She knows it's coming soon!"

She's referring to the marriage, but "soon" is a relative term in India. Kushboo remains behind the curtain while everyone else laughs and talks and stuffs themselves on mutton kebabs, chicken *biryani*, *naan*, cucumbers and dumplings.

Nicole's mother, Michelle, comes behind the curtain and tells us that she's signed the papers, so she's married now. She turns to Kushboo. "You're married now – congratulations!"

I can't tell from Kushboo's face what she feels. Married, and she's still never seen the groom. She murmurs something to Michelle. "She wants to see a picture of him. I don't think I should show her."

But a while later Leslie does. "What did she say?" we all ask.

"*Aacha* – okay," Leslie tells us.

"Well, as long as she's happy," Nicole repeats. "Or I shouldn't say 'happy' . . . satisfied."

"When is she going to meet him?" I wonder.

"Not until they leave at the very end," says Michelle.

I'm determined to stick it out; I want to be there for the unveiling. Finally, just before 1:00 AM, the women lead Kushboo out from behind the curtain, her face and form covered in her wide red *dupatta*. She sits in a chair on stage beside the groom, perfectly still while he wipes his face. Various family members pose for photos with the new couple. Some peek under Kushboo's veil, but neither I nor the groom catch sight of her face. She's a little mound of red cloth, unmoving and faceless for every one of her wedding photos.

Finally, the matchmaker – the groom's aunt, a wide woman with a loud laugh – lifts up some long garlands of red and white flowers joined together like a curtain. Each of the important women touches her head to this curtain; then the matchmaker ties it around Kushboo's head. The flowers fall over her face, above the red cloth. Then on goes the semi-sheer black veil once again.

Everyone moves Kushboo to the edge of the stage. Suddenly, Mehaboob smiles and picks her up, swings her over his shoulder and carries her to the door. Everyone sings in Hindi as he sets her down. Camera lights pop all around. Kushboo is a stone – a black, still, silent rock – the most important woman here and the only one without a face or voice. A tide of laughter and movement surges around her little form standing in the doorway, waiting. Tears stream down Leslie's face.

Another of Kushboo's brothers picks her up. One of her little hands suddenly comes out from beneath the veil and clings to her brother's neck. I'm so caught up in this scene that the wedding car almost runs over my foot. Kushboo's brother stuffs her in the back, veil and all, and the groom gets in beside her, a female relative on her other side.

"Still not alone together," Michelle murmurs.

Nicole peers in the window. "She's crying."

Michelle reaches through the open front window and grasps Kushboo's hand. I want to pick her up like I were one of her brothers and carry her off into the night, to find her some handsome, romantic young man to fall in love with. I desperately wish the groom would put his arms around her to comfort her, but instead he just sits beside her awkwardly. They're married – they're going to his house to sleep together – they'll spend the rest of their lives together. And they've never spoken or touched, never even looked each other in the eyes.

"Poor little Kushboo," I think over and over.

I so hope he's kind to her. I saw him take a little child's hand in his, and I pin all my hopes on that, though I haven't seen him smile.

As Amy and Leslie and I walk home, we're not quite sure what to say.

"Oh boy, why did they have to make her marry someone so old?" Leslie says. "He probably can't even have kids."

How could I do what Kushboo has done – or rather, how could I have it done to me? Did she feel like she had any choice? Was she happy once the entire night? Is this bravery, or fear? I couldn't – I wouldn't – do it. I don't cry, but there's a tight ache in my head and an even bigger one in my chest.

⌒

On a map, Old Delhi squats like it's giving birth to New Delhi, which lies below it. Since I arrived in India, I've been eager to visit Old

Delhi's spice market on Chadni Chowk and the towers of the Red Fort palace. But everyone warns me not to go there alone.

Today, however, the day after the wedding, I'm crammed into a car with Michelle, Nicole, Amy, Leslie and four of Kushboo's siblings. We're going for a post-wedding party at Kushboo's new home in Old Delhi. I'm burning to see how she is.

When the road suddenly narrows, Nicole tells me, "This is one of the gates of Old Delhi."

Living in India is like being inside a cement mixer – Old Delhi even more so. Slabs of meat hang from butchers' doorways, goat heads and legs are piled on tables outside, still covered in hair. A boy pedals a bike with a wooden cart behind us, which contains a bird cage with a white dove. A brown goat with the longest ears I've ever seen stands on a pile of dirt and butts its head fondly into a woolly sheep. Ahead of us rises a huge set of stairs, above which are the white domes and minarets of a huge mosque.

"That's the Jama Masjid – the biggest mosque in India," Amy tells me.

Leslie nods. "During the festival of Eid, this street is filled with men praying."

We park on one side of the mosque. When we get out, Amy nudges me. "Cover your head, Liz." I quickly drape my *dupatta* over my curly hair; this is deep Muslim ground. We form a little procession of bicycle rickshaws; I sit beside Azmat and try not to slip off the slanted seat. We turn right into a narrow alley, the sky a pale slice of light overhead. The roads are only wide enough for scooters and bicycles here. The way slants down like a giant tongue, and we fly deeper and deeper down through the maze of houses and dirty little shops, into the belly of the city. If I got lost in here, I don't know how I could even begin to find my way out.

When the rickshaws stop, we duck out of the dark alley into a bright courtyard with doors on each side. We enter a door on the left and find ourselves in a small bedroom. The right wall is covered in dark, carved wood cabinetry, ceiling to floor. On one shelf is a stack of old books in Hindi script. On the left is a low bed covered in a deep red taffeta duvet embroidered with flowers. Over and around it hangs a crisscrossed netting of red flowers and white jasmine. Their heady fragrance fills the room.

The women sit all around the edge of the bed and face inward. Kushboo is in the middle, in a heavily embroidered red *salwar kameez*. The *dupatta* is draped over her hair, which hangs in a thick black curl over one shoulder. Kushboo barely looks at us when we come in. When she talks to Heena, she holds the *dupatta* back from her face, but she hardly speaks to anyone else, even when they put their face under hers and ask her questions. As the women chatter and laugh, Leslie translates snippets of their conversation for Amy and me. "They were asking her if she had sex last night, and how many times. Imagine being asked that."

I never do find out the answer to that question, but as we sit down on the floor of the courtyard for lunch – men on one side of the curtain, women on the other – I wonder. The groom comes to sit beside Kushboo, across from me, and I study his behaviour. Now and then he offers her water, or Wonder Bread spread thick with butter, but he never smiles. He's balding on top – definitely not thirty-one. After lunch, which pushes my ever-growing tolerance for spicy food, we go back into the bedroom and sit on the bed. The matchmaker laughs loudly as she goes to the cupboard to show us all the clothes the groom's family has given Kushboo. As one of the women pulls a sparkly green suit from the pile of plastic-wrapped cloth, Leslie translates: "They're saying Kushboo should wear green because it's the groom's favourite colour."

The matchmaker pulls suit after glittering suit from the cupboard: saffron, deep red, black with multi-coloured embroidery, rose fading into teal. Fifty-two suits in all.

Michelle sighs. "Oh Kushboo!"

Compared to Kushboo's former life, lived in a dingy apartment of three small rooms and two shared beds, this is incredible luxury. But no one will see Kushboo's face or new clothes outside the closed doors of her home.

One of Kushboo's new relatives, a thin-lipped woman whose dark arms and face are covered in blotches of pale skin, holds up a long black garment decorated with tiny square rhinestones and motions for Kushboo to stand. All the women look at her, their eyes dark with excitement. This is the first time Kushboo's ever worn a *burqa*. As her relative teaches her how to wrap the black cloth of the headpiece around her face so only her wide, kohl-lined eyes show, I'm surprised by the festival air that surrounds the lengthy procedure. This seems to be a practice run, however; after a while Kushboo takes the *burqa* off and sits back down on the bed.

Her new sister-in-law, a cheery, warm woman with a gap between her two front teeth, grabs a plastic container from the kitchen and begins to beat it like a drum. "Sing a song!" she urges me.

"*Nahi!*" I refuse, laughing.

She and the other Indian women start to sing instead: first "Twinkle, Twinkle, Little Star" in English then loud, raucous songs in Hindi. They laugh and clap in rhythm to the plastic drum.

Leslie claps too, then pauses to lean towards us. "They're singing, 'Kushboo will make the *roti*, Kushboo will wash the dishes. Kushboo will burn the *roti*, Kushboo will lose the soap.'"

Michelle says, "It's like the army. She'll start out doing everything, then work her way up."

Suddenly, half the women in the packed room begin to dance. They shake their wide hips and twist their hands like Bollywood stars and pull the reluctant ones onto their feet. We scream with laughter. I wonder if the men in the other room are bored. In the middle of the bed, Kushboo finally smiles.

En route

Subject: Night Bus from New Delhi
From: Jann Everard

The night bus leaves New Delhi for the Nepalese border at dusk, after several lengthy delays. We were told it would depart at mid-day – my partner Jim and I even lined up at one point – but three times we were ushered back to the concrete bunker that serves as a waiting room to swat at flies and towel the sweat from our skin. After the second delay, a westernized local man asked if we could keep an eye on the two Buddhist monks he was supposed to deliver to Nepal. He must have seen my eyes widen with suspicion because he was quick to assure us that the monks had tickets and money for food and water.

I'm relieved that the bus is finally moving. Someone told us that not only would it be late leaving the station, it would probably break down along the way. Be prepared for between twenty and forty hours of travel, he'd said, before you get away from these infernal delays. Since arriving in New Delhi, I've done nothing but wait – to change airline tickets, to make a call at the post office, to change money at the bank. Customer service has been slow and irritable. ("You should have been here when we opened at 12:00. *But you're open between noon and 4:00. I can't help you if you aren't here when we open at 12:00.*") After a week of this, I'm eager to get to Nepal. It's been three years since the last time I was there and fell in love with the place. I want to feel the same sense of wonder that I felt the first time, trekking off the beaten path, meeting old women who knocked the living insects off their firewood before lighting a match, listening to the snap of the prayer flags in the wind. Trite as it sounds, I crave the quiet majesty of the mountains, the raw contrast of white snow peaks against cerulean blue sky, so intense that it forces you to confront your beliefs about modernization – or suspend them.

I smile at the robed men – boys, really – sitting across the aisle, their heads shaven, each with a bare shoulder. I wonder whether they are as hot, sweaty and miserable in their maroon cloth as I am in my Indian cotton. Maybe they can cool themselves through meditation, or maybe they're just used to the humidity. Perhaps I can learn something about cooling myself from the inside out if I watch them closely, at least enough to get me through the next night and day, across the border and in sight of the Himalayan range. This Indian bus, with its video screen, powerful speakers and fetid air, represents everything I need to get away from: crowds, noise, heat.

I settle into my aisle seat. For some foreigners, the aisle seat is the most comfortable, but I'm short and don't need extra leg room. For me, comfort is guaranteed by the quality of my earplugs and the quantity of Gravol I have consumed, both necessary to dull the high-volume fight scenes of the inevitable Indian movie. I hunker down against the sticky fake leather and try to cut off any view of the flickering video. Jim leans against the window and snores. He can get comfortable anywhere. It's a mountain-climber thing. I don't have the knack. I'm a base-camp groupie. A mountain worshipper, but from the comfort of a tent.

There are a few other foreigners seated amongst the mostly Indian travellers – we've introduced ourselves over the dark-haired locals – an Israeli couple fresh from military service, a single British guy and two English teachers from Denmark who unknowingly advertise their newness to local bus travel by sitting on the back bench seat. They will soon find themselves wrenched in so tightly that they won't be able to uncross their legs without the cooperation of those seated on either side. The Israeli girl approaches me in the first hour looking for – her words – feminine hygiene products. She is formal and embarrassed to ask, but I don't have any with me and have to suggest she try the Danish teachers. I thank God I don't have to make this trip with my period and sympathize silently with Israeli-girl. I understand her loss of modesty, the loss of modesty all travellers experience as our stomachs, bowels and other inner workings fail us publicly.

I doze for the next few hours; Gravol never puts me out entirely. My eyelids crack open at intervals to take in the firefly dance of cigarettes along the roadside. Our passing headlights pick out bleached cotton, loose-wrapped around haunches that crouch beside meagre wares. I avoid making eye contact with the people outside, even when we slow for the stray dogs and chickens blocking the road. Nine months of travel in this part of the world has not made me immune to the sight of extreme poverty, but I have grown realistic. I know I won't make a difference by throwing *baksheesh* out the window or by buying a baggie of lime "soda" tied around a straw when we reach the next rest stop.

Jim nudges me awake, pantomimes that I should remove my earplugs. I do it with reluctance; the video blares. "I knew I recognized that guy from somewhere," he says, mentioning a name I don't recognize and gesturing to the Brit seated ahead of us. "He's a really well-known alpinist." Jim, an accomplished climber himself, can't believe his luck. I smile, happy that he has someone to pass the time with on this interminable trip, and let my cheek roll back onto his shoulder. Now and then he shifts and wakes me; the discussion about mountains between the two men is animated. The names of peaks are tossed between them like Hacky Sacks.

Hours and hours pass. We nibble on biscuits, sip tepid bottled water and splash scented alcohol to cool our skin and relieve us of the pervasive smell of spice-laden sweat. Discreetly we check and double-check our valuables. The humidity in the air and the bus vibrations eventually lull us both into a trancelike state until Al, the British climber, leans over the seat and prods Jim's arm. "Hey, mate, I don't have a photo for the entry visa. Give me one of yours, will you." The rustle in the bus suggests we are finally near the border.

"You've got to be kidding," I say, so loud that even the video watchers give me a quick glance. Al has thick curly hair, must be six foot, three inches tall and is clean-shaven. Jim is five-eight, with thinning hair and a beard. The heat, Gravol and sleeplessness make me paranoid. "Are you crazy? It'll never work. We'll get in a shit-load of trouble."

"It'll be fine." Al has the easy, conciliatory way of someone who has fully adapted to this part of the world. His head bobbles left-right-left, a local gesture that back home would roughly translate as a pat on the arm. "The Nepalese think we all look alike anyway. What do you say?" He gives me a look that is at once friendly and pitying. My quick rise to anger is such a typical western response. *See how calm I am in the face of this little predicament?* his look implies. *You should loosen up.*

The fact is I *am* afraid to be turned back at the border. A week earlier we'd arrived at the New Delhi airport without visas and were assigned a surly guard overnight until a Canadian official could sort us out. Sheepishly we'd explained to the consular representative that our arrival in New Delhi from Moscow had been unplanned – that we'd hoped to re-enter China from Tajikistan after two months at a climbing camp in the Pamir Mountains. Our Soviet visas had run out before new Chinese ones could be procured. We pleaded ignorance; the last time Jim had travelled to India, Canadians hadn't needed visas.

As I sit, tense and exhausted, Jim tosses Al a bandana for his hair and nods to me to hand over a photo from the stash in my money belt. Al winks and uses one of those expressions that North Americans can't get away with, like *no worries* or *don't fash yourself.*

I always find border crossings in out-of-the-way places nerve-wracking. Little men try to wield big power. Today, as I approach the uniformed officials at Sunauli, my behaviour in the line-up – nail-biting, hair-tugging, twitchiness – would set off alarm bells at any significant international border point. Al is ahead of us, my eyes glued to his crumpled passport.

An official thumbs open the document. His eyes move between Al and the photo as, smoothly, he palms into his pocket the several American tens Al has placed inside. Al saunters away, tucking his passport into his money belt. When it's our turn, Jim gives me a wink. More tens disappear. I am stunned at the nonchalance of the men but have to admire their understanding of the system. Within a few minutes we are both issued visas. We can chalk up this experience as another cultural anomaly, another story from the road.

While we wait for the others to be processed, Jim and I stand with our backs towards the guards. The border town is chaotic, not too different from Delhi, really. Al buys a mug of *chai*. Israeli-girl approaches another group of female travellers who have arrived on a different bus. I watch as she makes her own small transaction. The two young monks pass me on my right, catch my eye and steeple their hands together in acknowledgement that the commitment to deliver them to Nepal is fulfilled – *Namaste*. The boy monks look happy. Their robes ripple on a small breeze. The sweat on my skin evaporates. Although buildings block the view, and we're still far from the mountains, I can't help noticing: the boys and I are looking forward – and up.

Subject: Second-Class Sleeper

From: Leanne Leduc

It was above fifty degrees Celsius, and I was in Jaisalmer, Rajasthan, staying inside the old fort, which dominates the desert skyline. The fort was built in 1156 in the centre of the town, up on a hill for a better vantage over the enemy. The entire city, including the central fortress, is built of a yellow-sand colour material, surely made from the surrounding Thar Desert. From afar, the urbanization is almost completely camouflaged. But up close, when the late afternoon sun shines down on the ancient desert town, it glistens like a giant nugget of gold – hence the nickname the "Golden Fort." In the evenings, the brilliant crimson horizon backdrops traditional Rajasthanis in full desert regalia as they ride their camels, metres of brightly coloured silky fabric waving out behind them as they make their way into town.

The old fort of Jaisalmer has a complete working city inside, with narrow brick-paved lanes that meander beneath high arches. Tiny hole-in-the wall shops sell sickly sweet desserts and *lassis*, and frightening meat is laid out on the ground to sell. Donkeys with carts move items around the passageways, women carry large baskets of fresh-baked flat bread on their heads, men play stringed instruments for money, children run through the streets kicking at wicker grass balls, and the holy cow wanders around the labyrinth-like fortress, queen of it all. Some of the hotels are built right into the fort walls. My room was in one of the rounded corners, in a lookout watch tower. The walls are one metre thick; a small shuttered window opens out over the sprawling metropolis of sandy mud huts below. I would sit in that window daydreaming and dangling my feet high above the city rooftops. Looking out beyond the buildings at the undulating dunes that went on for as far as my eye could see, I imagined a time of royalty and battle. The hot desert wind blew through my hair, and I felt like a true desert princess.

But my time in the golden wonderland of Rajasthan had come to an end. I was to take a train back to central India. I had decided to wait for a night train in hopes the temperature might drop slightly, making the journey less torturous. I boarded a Second-Class Sleeper at around 10:00 PM; the train was relatively empty, which almost never happens in India, but the heat wave kept the locals from travelling. Sleeper trains are the best way to travel in India. They have compartments with six bunks, three on each side. The bunks are one on top of the other, with a ladder at the end to access the top bunks. The beds are nothing fancy, just a slightly padded metal slab, covered in vinyl. A quick clean with a baby wipe, your own sheet, your pack for a pillow, and they are actually pretty comfortable.

After boarding the train, I found my seat/bed, and there was only me and one man in the compartment made for six. The man was a bit undesirable – short and troll-like, with a pointy face, bad body odour and slick greased-back hair. When he saw I was in his compartment, and that we were alone, he got a sleazy, conniving kind of look in his eyes. I did not feel truly threatened by him – I was twice his size – just slightly grossed out. I took my place on a top bunk, and the creepy man was on the bottom bunk, on the other side. He tried, through hand gestures and broken English, to ask me to sleep on the other bottom bunk. Despite the fact that that bunk would surely be much more comfortable, I did not oblige. I did not want to give him any mixed messages, which can happen very easily to a single woman travelling alone in India.

I climbed up the metal ladder away from the open window and slightly cooling breeze, into the stifling heat and constant bright light from the blinding lamps directly over my face. I tried to sleep for a couple of hours, but the heat was unbearable and the light obnoxiously bright. My "travel mate" on the low bunk seemed to be quite comfortable, snoring away.

After a couple of sleepless hours, I felt I had put in a good effort on that top bunk, so I decided to move to the low bunk, across from the creepy man. Besides, he was asleep, and I needed to get some rest. Down I climbed and quietly made myself comfortable on the other low bunk. The cool midnight breeze blew in the open window, the annoying floodlight ceiling lamps were blocked by the upper bunks, and I settled in easily. I soon drifted off to sleep with the white noise of the train clanking along to drown out my neighbour's snoring.

I was sleeping away when I was suddenly awakened, with a terrible start. I was totally confused and disoriented, and I could hear the creepy man saying, "Hello, hello lady, helloooo, you like?"

Between the bunks there was about a sixty- to seventy-centimetre gap. I had rolled off my bunk and had fallen to the floor. This was, by no means, the worst part. During my sleepy fall I had automatically put my hands out to the sides. Now on my side, I had grasped for a handhold and found an empty bunk, but on the other side my hand had found, and grabbed, with full force, a perfect hold . . . that's right, you guessed it, a full handful of creepy-man ass. I had a firm grasp on one full butt cheek. When I realized this, I was jolted from my dazed state, let go of his butt, jumped up and was back on the top bunk before I knew it, just trying to pretend those last few minutes of my life had not happened.

Unfortunately, I still had another eight or so hours to ride. Let's just say it took every bit of patience I had to ward off the multiple unwanted advances from the troll beneath my bed.

Ironically, my final destination was the world heritage site of Khajuraho and the ancient Hindu and Jain temples there. They are famous for their many erotic sculptures that inspired the Kama Sutra sex books. The temples contain hundreds of hand-carved statues depicting people in different sex positions with the opposite sex, the same sex, animals . . . the works. Perhaps my travel partner that night knew my destination and, because of my "forward advances" in the dark, thought I was just another sex-crazed western woman, just like all the ones he had seen in the movies.

THE NORTH

Subject: The Holy Man
From: Jennifer Waescher

By the time I got to the little river just outside Maharishi Mahesh Yogi's ashram, I was soaked in sweat. Whoever said don't go to India in August may have been right. But still, I was glad to be there, even in the monsoon season. There I was standing by a small river in Rishikesh; in front of me, a big group of *sadhus* were washing things in the bubbling brook, no deeper than my ankles.

They all wore the customary orange swaths, which, at that time of year in Rishikesh, could be seen everywhere in town on the many pilgrims making their journey to the foothills of the Himalayas and to the crisp, cool water of the Ganges, or the *Ganga*, as most Indians call the massive sacred river of Mother India.

It was hard to say, at a glance, which of these seemingly holy men were actually holy. Rishikesh was a holy town for pilgrims and also rife with scam artists for the desperate spiritual seeker. I was not desperate. I was at this particular spot because I had been told that just up the hill and behind the gates was the abandoned, and now overgrown, infamous "Beatles' Ashram." The place that the famous foursome ventured to in the 1960s, the experience of which subsequently changed their music and lives, and much of western culture in general thereafter.

It was worth a look, I thought.

With my T-shirt stuck to my body with sweat, and avoiding the eyes of lascivious onlookers, I braved my way past the bathing *swamis*. Before I could get far, one bearded holy man approached me.

"Hello? Hello? Miss? Where are you from?" His overly friendly voice echoed the classic opening line of all con men in India. I flinched. Having had to ward off all kinds of con men and would-be gropers for weeks, I was prone to tense up at any friendly approach. Reluctantly I answered. I hadn't yet figured out how to avoid those potentially frustrating encounters.

"Uh . . . Canada," I said.

"Oh! Canada!" His eyes lit up with the glee of someone having hit the jackpot.

Shit! I thought. Why was I so honest? Why didn't I say Turkey, or Bosnia? I could pass for a member of one of those countries. Why did I always say the oh-so-rich country I was really from? Especially when I hadn't actually been to my country in almost two years at that point.

"Oh, Canada is a beautiful country!" He said, smiling, head wobbling from side to side.

"Yes," I said plainly. Then I loosened my shoulders in shame. Why was I so on guard? Maybe this guy was just a nice guy, curious about me and my culture. I felt guilty, the western guilt that comes along with travel in third-world countries, and for being so resistant to a simple friendly gesture in a country where so many are so poor, and I really *was* the rich traveller.

"Yes, it is," I said, a little friendlier, and smiled.

"Have you been long in Rishikesh, Miss?"

"Not long, no, just a week or so."

"Oh! Then you must be needing someone to show you around."

Bingo. There it was.

"You know, you should be coming with me today, Miss. I will show you all of the beautiful Rishikesh, and you pay me with your Canadian money at end of the day, yes?" He moved towards me to grab my arm. I stepped back quickly. A *sadhu* tour guide? Talk about spoiling the illusion. At least he could have pretended to be spiritual.

"Oh no, I don't need a guide, thanks." I began to walk away.

"Yes, yes. You come now. Yes?" He tried to grab my arm again. This time I sprinted away, not answering. I left him hollering after me, as I jumped rocks over the stream towards the ashram.

There were many moments like that one, travelling in India, when I really had to summon up some awe from within, to see past some of the dodgier parts of being there. Because, truly, there are so many things about the place that do inspire some sense of reverence and awe for humanity – but the con man *sadhus* are not one of them.

A few moments later, I found myself standing before a locked gate. I had been told that the gate would be locked, and I'd have to find the side entrance. So I made my way round to one side, which had a gravel path heading up the side of the hill. Still dripping in sweat, I began the uphill ascent. It took ten minutes or so, and I found a dead end – a brick wall, and I couldn't see where else to go. A man appeared from behind a bush, an older Indian man with very long black hair. I worried for a moment that he was some kind of security guard. I was, after all, trespassing. He frowned at me and said something in Hindi. I tried to communicate that I was looking for the Beatles' Ashram.

He gruffly pointed in the direction of what looked like another dead end and walked off. I continued around the wall and noticed another path heading up. It was heavily covered with twig-like bushes. Perplexed, I realized the only way in was going to be through the bushes. The travellers I'd met earlier told me that they had just walked up a paved hill and carried guitars with them. But I couldn't see any other way. And I'd come that far. Letting go of a big sigh, and the idea of anything being easy in India, I ventured in.

I headed up the steep slope, pushed my way through the rough bushes, trying hard not to get any twigs in my eyes. On the other side, there was another wall, the wall of a small round building. I had made it inside the grounds of the ashram.

It was unlike any ashram I had seen so far in India. An ashram is a retreat centre, so to speak, with a guru that offers a particular bent on enlightenment. At an ashram, disciples of a guru meditate, chant, practice yoga, study holy scriptures and listen to lectures and teachings of the guru, typically. The buildings are often just a few humble lodgings.

My footsteps seemed to echo. The site was massive, and huge tree branches entwined above me. The many pathways, overgrown with weeds, went in all directions. I didn't know why the ashram had closed down or why no one had ever renovated it. It was a beautiful secret garden. A little wonderland, serene, quiet in the midst of the madness that was India. And no one else was around. Or so I hoped, suddenly afraid of being followed. My adventurous spirit had strengthened in my travels, as did my increasingly peculiar situations, so I chose to ignore the panic and listen to the deeper mantra always running as an undercurrent: just do it, don't fear.

I looked for the buildings my friends had described and that I'd seen in their pictures. I came across one almost right away. A small building with lots of big windows, now smashed in from weather, I supposed, or vandals. I walked into a big room with a stage at one end. It might have been the yoga or meditation hall. Sunlight gleamed through the windows, illuminating the inscriptions on the walls made by visitors over the years. Every last inch was covered. I smiled, thinking of all the travellers that had stood where I was standing.

It was a beautiful chamber of ghosts of travellers' past. Travellers that had braved the land of Mother India, with all her glorious and horrific spectacles of life that either repulse or lure people into a lifelong love affair – a tumultuous love affair with the overly crowded streets, the holy cows at every corner, their feces under foot; with the openness of death, decay, life and celebration, poverty and wealth; with the cacophonous splendour of it all, where comfort is a stretch of the imagination.

As I walked around the dilapidated meditation hall, I felt a part of something. I could almost hear people playing guitars and singing Beatles' hits in tribute to the band and the freedom of the hippie era. And India.

I wasn't sure where I was on the spectrum of love and hate with India at that moment. It changed continually as I moved through the place that was so different from anything I'd ever known before stepping foot there. I didn't know that my affair had already begun. As it had for other travellers trespassing in the old ashram, a sacred haven for foreigners in India. The place where we all whispered, "What am I doing here?" and half expected someone or something to answer back.

And then someone did.

"What do you mean 'here'? The ashram or India?"

I jumped out of my sweaty skin.

"Oh!"

I turned around to see a young man standing in the doorway.

"Sorry, I didn't mean to scare you," he smiled.

He was Indian. But not Indian from India. From some other place, a traveller like me. His hair was longish, falling over his ears, and he wore similar clothing to all of us backpackers. Loose and flowing.

"Um, well, it's okay," I stuttered, still catching my breath, and feeling disappointed that I no longer had the place to myself.

"What are you doing in India anyway?" he asked, coming closer.

"What?" I asked, surprised by the question.

"Oh, I'm just curious. I'm always curious about why people come here. It's not exactly Disneyland."

"Uh – well," I began, and then stopped.

"Sorry, that was rude of me, let me introduce myself first." We shook hands, asked each other the requisite traveller questions, and, true to backpacking nature, we felt comfortable and friendly within a few minutes.

"Let me show you the best part about this place." He led me out of the yoga hall, and we walked around some more dilapidated old buildings with smashed-in windows.

"This is the old dormitory," he said. "Can you imagine? The Beatles actually slept here." We walked through the old rooms, and then he led me up the stairs to the rooftop.

"This is the best part." He smiled.

The rooftop was unique, offering a beautiful view over much of Rishikesh, and featuring strange egg-shaped enclaves that were hollow on the inside. We walked over to one. It was like a large egg, split in half, the top half placed on the roof.

"What is this?" I asked.

"A meditation cave," he said. We went inside.

"Oh ... strange," I said.

"Let's sit." He gestured, and we sat down on the ground inside the "egg" and crossed our legs.

"Do you meditate?" he asked.

"Yes," I answered. And I did. I had begun meditating regularly, so it felt especially interesting to be in the meditation egg, there in Rishikesh. Somehow meaningful.

Egg. Birth. Conception. Life. There was a poem somewhere in there.

He faced me and looked into my eyes, sitting still for a moment. He was very calm and sure of himself.

I noticed his clothing remained sweat-free, an amazing feat, and he wore a colourful hand-woven bracelet on his right wrist. I was about to ask him where I could get one, and then he spoke.

"Good. Why don't we try it now? Together. Is that something you'd be into?"

I pondered his question only briefly. In the past I would have gotten up and ran away. Actually, more accurately, in the past, I wouldn't have found myself sitting in a meditation egg in northern India, in the middle of the day. So, the reference point was way off the mark. I had passed so many points of no return that I had stopped counting. My travels both outward and inward had brought me to strange and wonderful places, and the question placed before me at that moment no longer had any residue of the strange or suspicious. My defences for these things had long ago begun to drop away, and as I made my way on my peculiar journey, my willingness to surrender to life, and the situations it presented me, grew. As did my eagerness simply to live and experience.

Not that I put myself in danger unnecessarily. My intuition for what was genuine and sincere had been heightened, and this was one of those times.

"Yes. Let's try it," I said quickly. Why not? Why not meditate in an egg near the Ganges River, in the overgrown, abandoned "Beatles' Ashram" on a sunny afternoon?

So we did.

Two strangers sat quietly, cross-legged, facing each other, eyes closed and breathing.

Letting go of discomfort, the heat, the smells, the itches and just breathing. Sensing the breath of the other only slightly.

Something as seemingly simple as just relaxing and letting go was not easy, and normally it was more of a struggle. But that day, with all the right moments leading me up to that one, in just the right place and time, I felt myself let go. I felt many tensions and fears and struggles temporarily suspend in the air somewhere outside of me, and I began to swim in the relief that comes from such an experience. The sheer high of it. Of weight lifted.

Although my eyes were closed I began to see strange flashes of light, and I wasn't sure what to make of them. Heat stroke? Was I about to faint? An oncoming migraine? I sat and waited to see what would happen. Nothing happened.

After some time I felt ready to come out of it and return to the world, complete, not knowing how long I had been sitting there. I opened my eyes.

My new friend was gone.

I had mildly forgotten about him in the deep calm I had experienced, but now I was shocked that I hadn't heard him get up and leave. We had been sitting so close.

"Weird," I whispered, labelling it just another odd travel moment, when people come into and out of your life in intense bursts. Though it had seemed like more than that. That time, it had seemed more relevant for me in some way. Why had he wanted me to meditate with him, only to get up and walk away? Why hadn't I noticed?

I walked around on the roof, looking at the ground. I couldn't see him anywhere. He had totally taken off. I climbed the little ladder on the side of the egg to sit at the peak. The view was amazing. I took it all in but couldn't shake the strange feeling that had rolled in.

Eventually, I continued to explore the ashram, taking some photos, and made my way to leave.

I then realized I was lost.

I couldn't remember the secret entrance I had used to get in. I went to the main entrance, but it was locked, and there was no way to get over the high iron gate. A little surge of panic rushed through my chest.

I calmed myself, knowing I must be able to find my way out. The next half hour or so I spent frantically climbing through overgrown bushes on a search for my exit, only to find walls behind all of them. After collecting several scratches and scrapes and a newly sweat-soaked shirt, I stood in the middle of the ashram staring at the sky.

"What the HELL?" I yelled up. "Is this for REAL? Am I really stuck in this goddamn place?" All my former calm had vanished, and I dropped down on the ground, exhausted, frustrated and bewildered.

True to the theme of that day, my thoughts voiced to the sky yielded some kind of surprise feedback. Out from behind a little hut wandered an old *sadhu*. I stared at him aggressively as he quietly looked at me in my rather wretched state. What I did not want right then was a swindling con man disguised as a wise man.

"What's with this place?" I finally said to him, after we stared at each other for a few moments, assuming he wouldn't understand me. "What's with people appearing and disappearing? I mean, what the hell?"

He quietly looked at me, a small grin appearing on his lips. My frustration mounted.

"Okay, you know what? I'm going to get up and walk away, and please don't follow me. I do not need a tour guide. I do not need to buy any weird knick-knacks; I just need to get out of here. I am so done with this place now." I stood up and looked around, unsure what to do. I had already tried each direction. The *sadhu* watched me silently.

"Okay, actually, I do need a guide. But only to get out of here. Okay? I'll pay you to get me to the exit, and that's all I need. How about that?" I asked, a little calmer. He only smiled in response, and I wondered if maybe this one was the real deal. He finally gestured for me to follow him, and I sighed, relieved. He walked incredibly slowly, and when I got closer to him, I noticed he was very old. He must have been in his nineties.

He led me to what now, in hindsight, was the obvious way out that my friends had described to me. I don't know how I had missed it. He stopped at the edge of the ashram and gestured to the way out. I bowed in *Namaste* for thanks and tried to offer him some money, but he wouldn't take it. I smiled in recognition of a real holy man. He reached out his hand, and I held out mine, and when our hands touched, the strangest thing happened.

Looking back now, I still can't fathom how or why, or even what, happened. The same sense of total calm I had felt in the meditation cave came over me, the same light across my eyes. For a few seconds, it felt as though I was transported to another realm. I had read about how some people experience something like this in the presence of a real *sadhu*, or guru, or enlightened being. The act of holding his hand seemed to literally suck all the frustration away, and I sighed.

I looked down at his withered hand holding mine and noticed two things. First, I was crying. I hadn't felt the tears falling down my face until I tried to focus my eyes. Second, he wore a hand-woven coloured string bracelet on his right wrist.

Perhaps they were just popular bracelets, and many people in town had them, or maybe this old *sadhu* had led my friend out as well, and he had given the old *sadhu* his bracelet.

Those were certainly logical explanations. And my rational mind held on to those, even as a deeper part of me had a sense that something mystical hid within the coincidence.

The old *sadhu* released my hand, touched my face and wiped my tears, which hadn't stopped flowing though I wore a massive smile. He gestured *Namaste* and then took off the bracelet and handed it to me. I put it on right away. He made his way back into the ashram slowly.

I turned around to see India waiting.

The hustle and bustle, the heat, the merchants, the con men, all of it.

Though the colour of it all was just, if ever so slightly, brighter than before.

Subject: The Road to Bansi

From: Beverley Reid

It was well after 1:00 AM when our 747 from Heathrow touched down at Indira Ghandi International in New Delhi. The day had been a long one that began hours and time zones earlier in Vancouver. There were five of us – a three-person film crew, the subject of the film, whom I will refer to as "the missionary," and her travelling companion.

I had first become aware of the missionary a year earlier when her niece left a package on my doorstep. "I've seen one of your other films," the attached note read, "and I want you to do the same one about my aunt in India." The package contained a well-worn book, the autobiography of the Scottish-Canadian missionary.

I gave the niece a courtesy call back, intending to delay her until I had a chance to look at the book and think about her idea. I told her that I was in the middle of another film, that mounting a documentary usually took me about eighteen months and that the funding was very hard to come by. She was not to be discouraged.

"Don't worry, we'll find the money," she said. "My aunt is eighty-eight now so we need to act quickly."

My curiosity got the better of me, and I sat down to read the book soon after. A nurse in northern India for over sixty years, the missionary had founded a clinic for Hindi and Muslim women in a remote and isolated community. It was there, early in her career, that she had lost a leg to gangrene, the result of a freak accident. Against all odds she had recovered, and now, as an octogenarian, her work continued. I wanted to meet her.

I arrived at her small bungalow in New Westminster, B.C., early one afternoon. She was in Canada for a few months to avoid the monsoon season and the flooding of her clinic. She called to me as I knocked on the door, and I entered to find her sitting in a well-worn green velvet armchair, surrounded by piles of books. She was a small white-haired woman whose bright blue eyes flashed with a youthfulness and vitality I hadn't expected. Her voice was that of a young girl. Her interest in me equalled mine in her, and I had a hard time persuading her to talk about herself. When she did, the stories were compelling. Fluent in both Hindi and Urdu, she often had to pause to recall the "English" word.

My one-hour visit turned into two, then three, and the sun was setting when we said our goodbyes. As I drove back to Vancouver, I knew that there was a film here, and somehow I had to find a way to make it happen.

༠

In the year since that meeting, the niece and I had become fast friends, devising ways to raise money over many late-night cups of tea. I prepared a brief description of the film, which the niece sent with a personal note to the missionary's army of supporters. I took a more detailed proposal to the Banff Television Festival in an attempt to interest Canadian broadcasters.

Surprisingly, support for the film was immediate, and in less than three months, I was ready to finalize plans for a two-week shoot in India. In conversations with the missionary, I learned about the village of Bansi where the clinic was based and the surrounding community. I heard that accommodations for foreigners were non-existent and that food was scarce. The missionary confidently assured me that everything would work out and that I needn't worry. I believed her, but was uneasy nonetheless.

I focused on the logistics of the shoot. As the director and producer, I was counting on my husband Peter, an accomplished cinematographer, and Big Jeff, a towering man of many talents who would record the audio and double as production manager. First of all, though, I had several immediate problems. I needed to rent camera and sound equipment in India and to hire a bilingual camera assistant. I also had to figure out just how we were going to travel to Bansi, a two-day journey by train and jeep from New Delhi. Fortunately, these problems were quickly solved. Big Jeff discovered a film production house in New Delhi that could help us out. The missionary, with a couple of overseas calls, was able to make tentative arrangements for our transportation as well as her own.

I felt that we were as ready as we'd ever be.

On the eve of our departure, we gathered at the missionary's home. She was being interviewed and photographed for the *New Westminster Record*, her local newspaper, and was in fine form. She alerted us to the dangers ahead. "Always shake your shoes out before putting them on. Tarantulas, you know," she cautioned. "And don't disturb the cobras." The reporter mentioned that there had recently been brutal violence against foreigners in northern India, to which she flippantly replied, "Yes, I know, so let's hope we're not all slaughtered!"

While the missionary was interviewed, several of her friends filled suitcase after suitcase with supplies. I watched in amazement as canned goods, dry goods and perishables, including slabs of bologna and coils of garlic sausage, were packed for the trip ahead. The scene clearly underlined the many stories I had been told about the challenges we would face in Bansi.

I made arrangements for us to meet at the Vancouver International Airport the next day at noon. By the time everyone had checked in, we were travelling with sixteen suitcases and boxes, a wheelchair and numerous pieces of carry-on luggage. The missionary's niece was there to see us off.

"Well," she smiled at me, "we did it! Now you just have to go and get that documentary."

I laughed as I turned towards the departure gate. "Keep your fingers crossed," I called. "And leave your phone turned on!"

⌒

A fiery golden-red sun was setting as we loaded our luggage into a taxi van for the drive from the Blue Triangle YWCA to the New Delhi train station for our overnight journey on the Varanasi Express. The dusty narrow streets were clogged with pedestrians and traffic, and our progress was slow.

My time since our late-night arrival two days earlier had been taken up with finalizing the arrangements for the next leg of our journey. I quickly learned that even the simplest errand could take hours and had reluctantly spent one whole morning waiting in line at the train station to buy tickets. I visited the production house I had contacted from Vancouver and was able to rent equipment and hire a bilingual camera assistant, the very enthusiastic Darshan. I arranged to have him meet us at the railway station the next evening with the camera and audio gear, an additional six pieces of luggage.

It seemed that we were set, more or less.

As we inched into the station, the scene was noisy and chaotic. Vehicles were lined up for blocks as passengers laden with luggage dashed between them. We moved forward through food stalls offering the aroma of *pakoras, chapati*s, fruit and an array of tempting sweets. The driver suddenly stopped. "This is it," he said. "We walk from here."

We pushed out into the throngs and were surrounded by eager porters who grabbed aggressively at our belongings. Instantly, one, two, three and even four suitcases were loaded on heads covered by knotted bandanas. Monkeys chattered loudly as they scampered on the metal roof above our heads. We were besieged by ragged beggars and persistent vendors selling jewellery, bedspreads and housewares. The missionary was helped into her wheelchair, and with her companion clutching my arm, we moved towards the entrance archway. Miraculously, in the distance, we spotted Darshan who hurried to join us.

Our driver arranged for the missionary to be lifted over the many sets of tracks to our train. Pressed ahead by the surging crowd, the rest of us climbed a steep, interminably long flight of stairs to a large platform. Policemen with thick bamboo sticks struck out viciously at stragglers, and eventually, we reached the staircase leading down to our train. In the distance we could see the missionary waiting for us along with the numerous porters who were toting our luggage.

With much assistance, we were loaded into three compartments for the overnight trip to northeastern India and the small railway town of Basti. There we would disembark and transfer to jeeps for the five-hour drive to Bansi.

The sun was rising as the train screeched to a halt at the Basti station. Hundreds of anxious passengers lined the platform and rushed towards the compartment doors. I truly wondered how we would ever get off the train. We had only moments to get ourselves and all our luggage to safety before a whistle sounded and the Varanasi Express was on its way once again.

But with Big Jeff pushing the missionary in her wheelchair and the rest of us pulling wooden carts full of our belongings, we made our way outside, where two jeeps and drivers waited. We drove slowly through the grim streets of Basti, our luggage stacked perilously high on the jeep roofs, and out into the countryside. Village after village came and went as people, dogs and chickens raced to get out of our way. Again and again we were surrounded by fluorescent green rice paddies and fish ponds where groups of men plied colourful red and blue nets. Women in shimmering gold, orange and purple *saris* walked along the roadsides balancing huge water jugs on their heads as numerous cyclists caught up and passed them.

As we approached Bansi through a massive grove of mango trees, the missionary was full of excitement. "When I used to drive through these trees years ago, I'd pretend that they were all mine," she said, "and I knew I was getting close to home." We passed shops and roadside cafés that were full of men, and I noticed that there was not a single woman to be seen anywhere.

We drove on over a bumpy, red dirt road trailing clouds of dust before the jeeps slowed to a stop in front of an exotic-looking low building, the missionary's home and clinic. Surrounded by dense tropical vegetation with one lone palm tree, the brick and concrete structure was wrapped in a darkly screened porch through which our baggage was carried. Led by the missionary and her companion, the four of us followed.

We stepped into blackness. Doors were flung open, and as the daylight filtered through, my eyes gradually made out the contours of the room. Every surface was covered in layers and layers of dust, and the smell of mildew was overwhelming. Although it was mid-afternoon, we began to light kerosene lamps and to seek out the flashlights we had packed.

I realized that before any thought could be given to the film, the missionary's home would have to be made livable. Peter, Big Jeff and I changed into old clothes and started to scrub and sweep. It was a daunting task, and three hours into it, we could see little progress. I had managed to wash dishes and cutlery in anticipation of an evening meal even though I had no idea what we would be eating. I also had no idea where we would be staying.

Word of the missionary's arrival had spread quickly and soon a formidable looking gentleman who introduced himself as "the mayor" entered the house. This was a man who could make things happen, and persuaded by the missionary, he agreed to let us spend the night at the local Hindi guest house. The guest house provided shelter only, and if we required bedding, it was up to us to find it.

As twilight fell, Big Jeff and Darshan set off hoping to buy food from one of the dusty stands we had seen on the road. Peter and I hired a rickshaw to take us into Bansi proper in search of blankets. By the time we all returned to the clinic, we had a few *pakoras* and some vegetables but no bedding whatsoever.

After a very simple meal, we said goodnight to the missionary and her companion and walked through the darkened village towards the guest house, a clean basic concrete structure barren of any furniture and with no electricity. As the sun set, I sat on the floor by candlelight pondering this trip to Bansi and the upcoming shoot, which seemed to be getting farther and farther away. It was 7:00 PM.

The arrangement with the mayor had been that we could stay at the guest house for one night only, so as dawn broke and the muezzin's call to worship echoed over the rooftops early the next morning, I had still not solved our accommodation problem. We wandered back down the road to the clinic, struck by the beautiful mist which hung over the trees and obscured the terracotta buildings of Bansi. I was most anxious to get started, but it was clear that there would be no filming again today. The clinic had to be scrubbed and organized before the missionary could think of seeing any patients, and the rest of the house was still in need of further work. I also had to figure out, once and for all, where we would stay for the next two weeks.

The missionary had a simple solution.

"Well," she said, "you can all just stay here with me in the clinic."

"But you haven't space for the four of us."

"There's a nice little room behind the wall," she pointed. "I think you can be comfortable in there."

Carefully, I opened an ancient wooden door, loose from its hinges. Before me stood a small, filthy room, overrun by rats. A single bed was pushed against a wall; a dirty mattress lay on the floor. Two rough hemp cots which had languished outside for years had been pulled inside. In the absence of any other alternative, I made the decision that we would do our best to clean the room up and stay put. Later, we ventured into the village and bought four blankets. We were now officially on location.

After dinner two days later, with the house finally in order and the clinic ready to receive its first patients, I sat down with the missionary to talk about the film.

That night, the four of us stood outside. It was pitch black, the only light coming from a crescent moon silhouetted behind a solitary palm tree. We wanted to toast the upcoming shoot. In the absence of any glasses, we had made our own from cut-off water bottles and empty pill containers. As we raised these "glasses" to the sky, we paused to reflect on everything that had happened and our good luck in getting this far. We were in a magical place, and in that moment, we all knew it.

RAJASTHAN

Subject: Palace of Winds
From: Sarah Mian

My Friends,

India has tied me up with silken ropes, and I am a model prisoner. Right now I am lying on my back listening to the smooth collapse of night onto the rooftops while the monsoon dashes shadow-drops against my wall. My lover has not been back for hours, but the smell of him remains. Sweet, grassy, not at all like the others.

I have many little rituals here. I stroke my eyes with gold shadow, rub scented petals into my feet, buy fresh undergarments every day and throw the old ones away. I snap a picture of myself in bed just before he arrives and again after he leaves.

Hovering over the Pink City is a sandstone castle called Hawa Mahal, the Palace of Winds. Its thousands of odd-shaped windows were cleverly constructed to allow princesses to gaze out and observe the lower class without being seen themselves. This castle haunts me. If I even think of it, for weeks I cannot wash its image from my mind.

Yesterday I strolled along the bobbing eyes of the marketplace, barely resisting the childish urge to trail my fingers in the baskets of yellow spices and suck on them, yank the embroidered purple blankets down from their ropes, violently squash the tiny black beasts that scurry underfoot. Carts and quarrels crisscrossed the path as my lover walked ten paces away with hands clasped low behind his back, a smile playing like a silent film upon his lips. When we could no longer stand it, he found a fissure between stalls. I followed, and in the cool muted blackness, he licked my teeth, my collarbone, my knees.

I have no Palace of Winds to conceal my secret. I have only the crack in the curtains to monitor his daily routine, the minutes crawling upon my skin. When we met I was standing with my feet in the water. He followed my gaze past the low fountain wall to the hills beyond and asked what I was searching for. I told him I don't have to search; everything finds me. He asked, Why then did I come to India? To hide, I confessed. He laughed and said I hide like an elephant under a bowl of rice.

I watched them once. They did not seem unhappy. He was holding his wife's elbow so tenderly, as if she would shatter if he pressed in even slightly with the tips of his fingers. They got into a car and drove away to a place my imagination painted with swaying mango trees and giant circular stars.

One day soon I will awake back home. I will look out over fields of crusted snow and shivering apple trees and will hardly believe that this Pink City exists under the same pale moon. I will wear boots and eat pot roast and watch plodding television news of power outages and container ships. I will not speak of the places I have squeezed myself or of the man who mauled my heart into a gasping, feral creature. But at night in my dreams I will return here, standing on his altar swathed in flies and fever and branding-iron kisses. Even now I feel his arm hair brush my breast as he leans to blow out the candles. There are five of them flickering in gold-painted pots. Now four. Three. Two. One.

Darkness.

I will have so much to tell you, my friends, but no more words. I will show you digital photographs that don't mean a thing. You will see that I am more lost than ever and vow never to wander past your own creaky, gaping gates.

Sarah

Subject: Bird Sanctuary
From: Heather Conn

Gee, even inside a 7,000-acre bird sanctuary in the state of Rajasthan, I have to fend off unwanted groping from a too-eager Indian man. But I'll get to the best part after I share the beauty. I've spent glorious days alone here, exploring Keoladeo National Park, a wetlands park and World Heritage Site near Bharatpur. I gawk at wildlife, either when I am walking or riding a rented, old-fashioned bicycle with no gears. With such warmth and sun, it's hard to believe that it's early December.

Among large clusters of mimosa trees, sprinkled with yellow blossoms, black cormorants weigh down branches, their outstretched wings drying as if pegged to a clothesline. On the top branches, farther away, storks and cranes perch, their whiteness the flush of starched laundry. I've even seen some rare Siberian white cranes: elegant birds, with long, spindly legs of scarlet and a dash of red on half their face. With only a hundred and fifty on the planet, they are the second most endangered bird in the world. Remarkably, this park has twelve; six apparently arrived the day before I saw them.

The cranes, so tall and serene within the acres of wild marsh, are a gift of silent grace amidst the brash, fluttered green of parakeets, the shrieking alarm call of a peacock (India's national bird) and the frenetic dips and darts of kingfishers shimmering in iridescent turquoise and copper feathers.

Today, a munching cow ignored me while what looked like two wild boars dashed across the road. Several others sprang away into green thickness. Two blue bull antelopes, resembling spotted deer, stared at me, then darted away, their tall racks a poise of points. I heard the haunting howl of a jackal and saw two on the road about fifteen feet away from me as I cycled past. They, too, stared at me. I had expected them to look like hyenas, but to my unscientific eyes, they seemed more a mix of fox and dog or mini-wolf. At dusk, the sky swam with pink light, dipping clouds onto the marsh water. Before the three-quarter moon appeared, silhouettes of storks floated on trees, bobbing against the disappearing pale blue of the dusk sky.

Away from the probing male eyes of urban India, I have relaxed, lost in the discovery of wildlife. Among these park animals, I have no fear, no concern about men's wayward hands or leering grins, so common in the cities. Here, I am not prey.

Yesterday afternoon, I started chatting with a thirtyish Brahmin man who serves as a professional bird watcher and guide for western tourist groups. His latest group was cancelled due to recent curfews and unrest in neighbouring Jaipur, so he offered to accompany me for bird spotting and identification. It was wonderful to benefit from the trained eyes of such a knowledgeable person. But he quickly became exasperated when I couldn't remember the names of birds, even after he told me repeatedly. Each time I got a name wrong, he rolled his eyes and clicked his tongue as if handing me a dunce cap. Finally, I told him that I did not come here to get tested, and he stopped quizzing me.

Fancying himself a jetsetter, he has tried to impress me with names of millionaire buddies and clients such as a British Tory member of parliament. He says that he is looking for a wife (a too-familiar line here) and has been involved with a British woman; of course, he has suggested that we could be together. The mention of my Indian lover, Mukesh, has made little difference to him. We've talked philosophy; he thinks of life as a struggle. Napoleon is his hero. He has held forth on Indian men's ignorance in sex and their cluelessness in relating to western women. Obviously, he doesn't include himself in this category. Several times, he has grabbed my shoulders and leaned in close to my face. Once, he pecked me on the cheek.

"Fuck off!" I told him, surprised at my vehemence. After too many months of fending off unwanted touching from men here, I've snapped. In many places in Rajasthan, I've ended up kicking or screaming at some lustful hawker to get him to leave me alone. I know that makes me sound like some out-of-control wacko. At first, I tried to ignore the inappropriate comments and rude gestures, but I admit that the accumulative harassment has gotten to me. So much for my attempt to emulate Gandhi's path of nonviolence.

I am amazed now at how lonely I must be feeling to agree to the company of this bird guide (bird dog?). Despite his ingratiating monologues and offensive insinuations, I stupidly agreed to share a beer with him last night at the park's tourist lodge. We walked back to my tourist bungalow, following the road lit by the moon.

At the bungalow, I ate a delicious dinner of fresh vegetable *thali*, prepared by the owner's wife, while the bird guide proceeded to get drunk on rum. The bungalow owner joined us, drinking whiskey, while I had a gin and Limca, India's carbonated lemonade. When we said goodbye, the guide tried to kiss me and wouldn't release me from a tight hug. After he pinched my ass, I felt truly disgusted.

Back in my room last night, I noted a red *bindi* stuck on the wall – you know those decorative, bright-coloured dots that Hindu women wear in the centre of their foreheads (the "third eye")? I looked at that dot and thought, Who knows? Maybe it symbolizes some proud conquest. It could be the start of an ongoing series, like a notched bedpost.

Before you think I've gone squirrelly from too much solo travel, let me tell you something else I've discovered in some Indian tourist bungalows. While taking a shower or undressing in one of these rooms, I've noticed obvious cracks or decayed areas in the walls. You're thinking, Yeah, that's typical of backpacker joints. I agree, and yet when I have looked at these areas more closely, I have found that some of them actually contain a peephole! Whether that's by accident or willful intention, I dunno, but it's creepy. Ever since I noticed an eyeball observing me indoors at a previous place, the first thing I do here when I walk into any overnight room is survey the walls for tell-tale holes and cover them up.

〇

The tourist bungalow owner lives in a large, comfortable home with a beautiful wife, two adorable children – a five-year-old girl and a three-year-old boy – a kitchen helper and a young boy who looks after the kids. He tells me that his mother chose his wife for him; he asked only to see his bride-to-be before they married, which he did from afar for about two minutes. He didn't want to get married but says that he is happy now. He wants to travel, to go to England, but his wife doesn't. She never joins our talks and seems to understand little English but appears to me to be a loving, independent-minded dynamo. The owner says that she has a mean temper, but I assume that it's probably justified in most cases.

After drinking too much whiskey, the owner confesses to an indiscretion with a married American tourist years earlier and expresses a similar interest in me. When I deflect his comments, he doesn't persist, thank goodness.

While staying at this tourist bungalow, I have learned that whiskey drinking around the fire is a frequent routine. One night, the owner's nephew summoned me to eat dinner inside his home, but when I got to the house, I saw that the owner wanted me to join the men for drinks. Since his family has shown me considerable hospitality and warmth during my few days of visit, I didn't want to offend their generosity.

As the men puffed on cigarettes, ate peanuts and scattered the shells on the floor, they talked almost exclusively in Hindi, ignoring me. I sat there, in silence, with no idea if they were discussing me; when they nodded in my direction, it seemed obvious. Here I was, supposedly one of the guys, while the rest of the family sat in another room. Why did the owner invite me to join this all-male group? Was it genuine conviviality or was he just another frustrated husband who wanted an affair and to live vicariously through our dialogue? Excluded from the conversation, I finally excused myself and left the room, feeling like an embodiment of the Other, an outsider by gender, language and nationality.

Like a magnet with shifting poles, I know that I represent a strange
duality for some Indian men: a buddy and confidante *and* a sexual target.
Young men who work here as outdoor guides for tourist groups,
for instance, are well exposed to westerners. They're grateful to talk
freely with me like an old pal, sharing frank views and topics deemed
unacceptable in mixed company within their own culture. However, I
have discovered that the line between such cozy camaraderie and an
unwanted gesture or assault is too thin.

⌒

In the owner's home, I wondered why the woman who waited on us
one night at dinner had her face covered by a veil. I found out later
that she was his sister-in-law and lived there. He told me that, due to
village custom, she could never speak or show her face in his presence,
since he's the family's eldest brother. He has no idea what she looks
like and has never even heard her voice. Before entering a room in his
own home, he has to announce his arrival to give her time to cover
herself. When she enters or leaves a room, she has to ensure that her
face stays hidden. Meanwhile, her husband wears western clothes,
speaks English and has travelled across India, Nepal and Pakistan.
And I thought that gender-defined behaviour in *my* culture was
limiting . . . .

When the owner drinks with friends indoors, his brother drinks
alone in another room, which I find strange. I learned another village
custom: a younger brother cannot drink with his older male sibling.
Instead, the owner's nephew serves as go-between, refilling the brother's
glass from the other room. Apparently, if two brothers move to the
city, they must still continue this tradition. In the meantime, Indian
women in the village certainly never drink with men.

I've been wondering if the owner is stringing me along about these
customs, but his family's behaviour seems to bear out what he tells
me. I can't ignore how gender has affected my treatment in India, yet
I have enviable freedoms compared to the women in this village.

I envy male friends from North America who can explore India's
streets alone at night without facing sexual or verbal assaults from this

nation's men. Some might say that if you think like a victim, you will be one; but the layers of male expectation and assumption here, especially towards a freckled, red-haired, white woman, underlie many conversations and experiences I have with Indian men, regardless of my thoughts or actions. I want to find connection with others here, regardless of gender, yet reminders of how men view my femaleness too often intrude.

Even with the women in India, I can't always escape stereotyping. Remember what happened when I visited the state of Sikkim in northeastern India? A female receptionist at a hotel mistook me for a prostitute, even though I had a scruffy backpack and wore a long, bulky wool sweater and hiking boots. A proud local resident, a civic official, had toured me around Gangktok, the capital, and suggested better accommodations than the dark, low-cost place I was in. When we appeared at the counter of his recommended hotel to inquire about room availability, the receptionist looked at this dignified, middle-aged Indian man, then at me, and assumed that we just wanted to have a quickie. Her assumption offended both of us, even though she apologized. When I walked alone at dusk in Gangktok, men spat at me and treated me as if I was topless, even though I again wore a thick sweater, hiking boots and long pants.

With such attitudes in India towards western women, I have pondered my possible future with Mukesh. How would my life unfold in this country, married to an Indian man who's never left the country, and living with him and his parents? Despite our differences in culture, race, nationality and age, Mukesh and I have seriously discussed what it might be like to endure daily scorn as a mixed-race, married couple within his country. Am I prepared to stay here with him? That choice does not feel right, yet I berate myself for not embracing it. *This must mean I don't love him enough.* Once I return home, we plan to have Mukesh immigrate to Canada.

Until then, can my rebel spirit endure his father's bizarrely misguided view of me as a corrupting older woman who brazenly travels unchaperoned and is bent on kidnapping his son, getting him hooked on heroin and then scuttling him off to Canada? Stay tuned.

Subject: Udaipur: A Love Story

From: Jasmine Yen

Udaipur is known as the most romantic city in India. Located in the mid-south part of the northwestern province of Rajasthan, it is a contrast to the wide deserts of the north and west. At its heart is the picturesque city palace, set on Lake Pichola. Canopied, white-washed boats ferry tourists between the palace and the various floating hotels.

I arrive in Udaipur after two weeks of travel through Rajasthan and am instantly in love with the city. After a chilly nine hours on a sleeper bus, I reach the bus depot, a signless point at the side of a road. Nothing opens in India before 10:00 AM, so the rickshaw ride through quiet streets is quick and brings me to my guesthouse in ten minutes. My room is not ready, so I make my way to the rooftop restaurant where I enjoy a huge breakfast of eggs, toast and hash browns (with *masala*, of course). My room ends up not being ready for three hours, so I read a newspaper and learn that people in India are also hysterical about swine flu.

Back at my guesthouse, my room is finally ready, and I am delighted to find both the room and the bathroom virtually spotless, though there is a curious stain on one of the pillows. I turn it over and am delighted once more. I am also exhausted after a sleepless night but excited to be in a new place – so excited that I decide to stay for a week.

The cough that I had before I left home has gotten worse, and I am beginning to worry that I have some sort of infection; so after unpacking, I venture outside to explore and look for a doctor. I ask a man if I am going the right way to the footbridge, and he confirms and strikes up a conversation. His name is Case and he is from Holland,

and this is his tenth journey to Udaipur. He knows everything about everything, and I very quickly discover that I do not like him at all, but he has attached himself to me and offers to take me to the government hospital, which he assures me is the best (because it is free). I politely decline his assistance, but he does not take the hint, and so I have a companion for the better part of the afternoon.

After much searching and several confusing conversations (Case has been to India over a dozen times, yet he doesn't speak a word of Hindi), we find the hospital. But of course it is closed. I am told to return at 5:00 PM. When I return, it is still closed. I ask around some more and am told that there is a private hospital, American Hospital, and that it is the best place to go, so I overpay a rickshaw driver to take me there.

I walk to the reception and am asked to fill out an admittance form. The first half is standard: name, age, birth date; but the second half asks for the information of the "person responsible." I ask if this is necessary and am told it is. So I put down my father's name, occupation, marital status (I lie and say he is married), religion (I lie again and say he is a Christian), address and phone number. I realize that in India I am not a person. This is unsettling. I pay a total of fifteen hundred rupees, which is equivalent to around thirty-five dollars, to see the doctor, have blood and phlegm tests and a chest X-ray, all without having to wait. I think that this is a phenomenal deal, but after three subsequent visits (during two of which I am told to return the next day) the doctor tells me that the tests are all fine and I should not drink cold water and I will be better. Of course! Why didn't I think of that? I've been coughing for three weeks because of cold water. I feel mildly ashamed at being ripped off yet again. Fortunately, my cough seems to be getting better on its own, but I hold onto my little bag of results (including my X-ray – a nifty souvenir) for consultation with a doctor in Delhi if I do not recover fully.

The hospital itself seems clean and fairly up to western standards, though I'm not entirely certain that the X-ray technician hasn't inappropriately felt me up a little, and while the nurse who takes my blood uses a brand new needle, she does not wear gloves and there is a small amount of other people's blood splattered on her desk.

The next morning I sleep late, and as I leave my room, I see Case standing at the bottom of the stairs. Has he been waiting for me? He smiles and waves and asks if I would like him to show me around some more. I am mildly horrified, and this time I am a little less polite when I tell him I would like to spend the day alone. Thankfully, he takes the hint and leaves fairly quickly.

I plan to walk a little then find a rickshaw to take to the hospital for my results. Outside my hotel, I am stopped by a man who pleasantly inquires, "Hello, what is your country?" This is the standard opening line of men trying to sell you something or fuck you (or both if they're really smooth). I ignore this inquiry eighty percent of the time, which might seem rude, but if I were to stop and answer everyone who inquired, "What is your country?" it would take me a whole morning just to make it one block, because this question will be followed by "What is your name?" "What is your job?" "What is your father's/mother's/brother's/sister's name?" and "You will have *chai* with me?" If *chai* is accepted, other questions one can expect are along the lines of "How long you are in India?" "What is your favourite thing in India?" "How much is your salary?" "I show you a special palace on my motorbike?" "Do you drink beer?" and always, "Are you married?" There is very little variation from this script.

I'm feeling rather jovial, so I stop to talk to the man. His name is Khan, and he is a shopkeeper and sells mostly pashminas. He assures me very quickly that he doesn't want to sell me anything or sleep with me, though he does not say this last part directly. Men here like to talk in code when it comes to sex. Standard come-ons include "I am very open/modern," "I like western ways," and my favourite, "I study at Osho" (a school of "yoga" known for its openness to sexuality). "I am not thinking like other men" is supposed to imply that they won't come on to me, though this has yet to actually prove to be true. Khan offers to drive me to the hospital, and I initially decline; but he is persistent, and I accept. I hop on the back of the motorbike with the stranger and go tearing through the streets of Udaipur – there are, of course, no helmets. Yet, as with all the precarious forms of transportation I have taken here, I feel oddly (and unreasonably) fearless.

This is one of my favourite things about Rajasthan: the friendliness. Perhaps I am experiencing a false sense of security, but accepting tea and getting motorbike rides from strangers have become standard practice. My first few days in India I ignored everyone, but once I stopped, I found myself meeting a lot of very kind people who were willing to show me around their towns, take me to their homes to meet their families, share food with me and provide helpful advice. Of course, I am not so ignorant as to believe that any of them did this without ulterior motives, but as I mentioned previously, I have felt entirely safe in India. And feminist sensibilities aside, I have (almost) shamelessly enjoyed the advantages of being female (free food/drinks/transportation, better seats on buses, acceptable line budging).

The slight bit of guilt I've felt over my blatant use of my gender comes from the many warnings I've read and had relayed to me about how western women perpetuate a negative image of themselves by acting inappropriately (i.e., talking with strange men, going on their motorbikes, drinking alcohol). I am back and forth on how I feel about this. On the one hand, I want to be a good representative of my country (I act respectably in other ways, like dressing appropriately, not swearing, not getting drunk), but on the other hand, I really like free stuff, and it's kind of nice to have people telling you how great you are, even when you know they're full of shit.

Khan, it turns out, is like most men. After the hospital stop, we ride into a national park and up the mountain to a castle – the "monsoon palace" – at the top. The view is exquisite. We sit in a tiny vestibule, looking down on the tiny town and lakes far below. Khan makes his move. And it is a unique one.

"I love you," he tells me.

"Oh," I respond.

Noticing my discomfort, he attempts to assure me, "This is special Indian love . . . not like in the west." He leans in to kiss me, and I lean away.

"I'm sorry. I have a boyfriend in Canada," I lie. But he's heard this before. He knows I'm lying.

It briefly crosses my mind that I've made a mistake, coming to a remote location in the middle of India with a strange man whom I've only known for three hours. But my gut was right, and Khan backs away.

Then he tries his second move. One that is new to me. He begins to cry.

"I love you so much. You are not understanding." And it's true, I'm not understanding. And I almost kiss him because I feel awkward and that would make it less awkward, but I don't, and I ask him to take me back to the hotel.

I spend most of the rest of the week with Khan. Rejecting him over and over again starts to feel a little cruel, so I buy one of his over-priced pashminas and tell him I don't mind if he tells his friends we had sex. After all, he's invested a lot of time in me.

For the most part, Udaipur is relaxing and lazy, but at times, even with Khan's companionship, it is a little lonely. The city is filled with tourists, but the vast majority doesn't speak English, and virtually everyone seems to be travelling as a couple (it's a romantic city). And while an afternoon spent trying to communicate with a Spanish- or German-speaking person can be somewhat enjoyable, it really just ends up being frustrating.

The real highlight of my week comes on day five: a day trip with a girl from Australia to Ranakpur, a two-hour drive from the city. She has used her feminine wiles to secure a car and driver at no cost, and I feel better about myself knowing that I am not the only one giving western women a bad name. I am also excited about more free stuff. The reason to visit Ranakpur is several Jain temples, set in a lush, jungly oasis in the desert (watering abuse is evident). The temples are incredible, the most impressive I've seen yet. The largest, cool and serene, has over one thousand marble columns, each one covered with intricate carvings of flowers, animals and people.

By day seven I am tired of Udaipur and ready to move on. The novelty of fending off men has worn off, and I am cranky and snap at several shopkeepers. I don't even want the free stuff anymore, so I opt to pay a woman, Minu, to take me around for the day. We met the evening before when I ate at her tiny restaurant. Encountering a local woman who speaks English and moonlights as an unofficial tour guide (I don't know if there are actually official guides) is unheard of, and I don't mind that I am overpaying to basically spend the day driving around with her while she does what she would do any other day. Her two children, ages three and six, join us, and the four of us climb onto her scooter (I've seen a family of seven on a bike, so four isn't really that many) and leisurely visit some gardens, shops, and both her sister's and brother's homes. The day is an enjoyable end to my week.

Subject: Pushkar Puja

From: Eufemia Fantetti

Pushkar is a Hindu holy pilgrimage town on the edge of the
Rajasthan Desert. The main thoroughfare, Sadar Bazaar Road, is
usually teeming with tourists, locals on motorcycles, beggars and
cows. The tourists move from vendor to vendor, shopping, eating and
avoiding. Early morning on my way to yoga class, it's another town
entirely, extremely quiet with only one *chai wallah* near the Lake
View Hotel continually calling out "Good morning Madam! *Chai?*"
There are a few folks sweeping the street, cleaning out the debris of
the day before, praying and taking care of over four hundred temples.

When I read about the number of temples in the guidebook I
thought, *This I gotta see.* I was picturing ornate splendour with a myriad
of my favourite gods and goddesses spilling out everywhere. But most
of the places of worship are simple and modest, tiny spaces the size
of closets, squished in between tiny restaurants that seat twelve and
clothing shops, some the size of three North American dressing
rooms put together. The sounds of bells and chanting mix with the
calling out from the people performing their *puja* (worshipful offerings)
and bathing rituals down by the holy Pushkar Lake. The legend of
the lake is that it sprang up "where lotus petals fell to the ground
from the flower carried by Lord Brahma." Gandhi's ashes are in that
lake.

Almost every day in Pushkar, some man will try to give me a carnation
and direct me to the lake. Just like that.

It makes me think of that ridiculous commercial from the 1980s for that spray cologne called Impulse, of all things. The commercial had a guy chasing after a woman to give her flowers after he had caught a whiff of her incredibly cheap but supposedly irresistible cologne. The voice-over said, "If a complete stranger suddenly gives you flowers, that's Impulse." I'd call that stalking, but then again, I have at times been accused of being unromantic. By several different people.

But here in Pushkar, I've been experiencing something between stalking and a "you're just the sucker I've been waiting for" attitude.

It's easy to have your suspicions aroused when they're so darn adamant that one should carry this flower down to the lake, and that it's vital, or one really isn't immersed in a Pushkar vibe; one is not experiencing the real India, is not progressing spiritually. My first day in town, the fellow who gave me the flower popped up three times from three different *ghat* entrances to say, "Hello, lake this way," and "Excuse me, this way is going to the lake."

It happened again on my second day when I was off to find the yoga class that Sarah, a fellow ashram escapee from Bihar, recommended. I left my room, waved and said *Namaste* to the hotel manager standing in the outdoor lobby. A fellow on the street noticed me, said something to the manager, whose reply was very short, and the next thing I knew, a flower was thrust into my hand.

My Hindi is really not improving at all. The *Hindi for Travellers* phrasebook purchase was a bust. There's no record of "Good morning" or "Good night," but I recently came across "Do you have a sister?"

I still managed to translate the exchange:

Guy from the street: "Is she new in town?"

Hotel manager: "You betcha."

This gentleman popped up at the next *ghat* entrance I passed, saying, "Madam, lake is this way." (You can't really miss Pushkar Lake; the town is built around it. You can only walk towards it or away from it. Usually, you are walking *around* it.)

I said "Yes, *dhanyavad*, I can't go right now."

He insisted I go; there was a festival on (if so, it was the quietest festival India has ever put on). "Now is best time going. You know what 'festival' means Madam?"

Gosh, no, I better check my phrasebook. Could it mean "Let's herd the foreigners down to the lake and put another one over on them?" Just a wild guess.

I tried again to explain I was in a rush; I had to find this class. "Sir, I don't understand why I have to go down to . . . ."

"Look here, there are three gods," he said, "Brahma . . . ."

In my impatience I said, "I know this, and there's Shiva and Vishnu, but why do I have to go to the lake? I don't mean any disrespect, but I don't understand the custom." And hey, I noticed the signs from day one here and took them very seriously. There will be no photographing, no shoes within thirty steps of the *ghats*, no inappropriate displays of affection from me.

The man said, "Okay, give me," and grabbed the flower out of my palm.

Fine by me. If a complete stranger suddenly gives you flowers, that's weird.

Later, I asked Sarah, "What's the deal with the flowers? Is that happening to you too?"

Sure was. In fact, she referred to it as, "Being *puja'd*."

Puja means *offering*. So you go wandering down to the lake, carnation in your outstretched palm, where some priest will find you. In fact, he's been waiting for you. He asks you to "Repeat after me," which she did, line for line, word for word, up until the part that went "I will make a donation." Then she walked away.

"Bad karma for you and your family," said the helpful priest.

Yesterday, on the way to yoga, I had a thirteen-year-old kid start following me. A freaking kid! He saw me, changed his course and intercepted my path. Actually, it would be more appropriate to say that he swaggered and tried to position himself right behind me. I stopped and glared at him, and the kid stopped for a moment, uncertain what to do.

A gentleman coming from the other direction said something to the kid in Hindi, and the boy went back to his side of the road. The man smiled at me and said as he walked past, "Sometimes, in India, too many problems."

I thanked him in Hindi and said in English, "You're right about that."

En route

Subject: Camel Rides and Weddings
From: Janis Harper

Our sleeper train to Udaipur, Rajasthan, was a difficult ride: the train was very narrow and felt like it could topple over at any moment, and the constant jostle and jump made my tiny upper berth a challenge to stay in, much less to sleep in. The metal grate between me and a man sleeping in the next berth didn't keep out his snores (or pungent breath!), and the large family beside us enjoyed chatting noisily all night, which is not uncommon on trains here.

But Udaipur was beautiful – a former kingdom, its lake, ringed by mountains, has the majestic Jagminder palace "floating" on it; the huge city palace complex, fairytale-like, on its banks; and the unfinished "monsoon palace" high on a hill. These palaces, and Udaipur itself, is the setting for the classic James Bond movie, *Octopussy* – and almost every restaurant here shows the movie in the evening, every evening. Adam got sick for a few days while I roamed the streets, drank *chai* and talked with various locals, including a woman who proudly invited me to see her one-room house. (We sat on a stack of mattresses while her daughter-in-law squatted on the floor by the stove to make our *chai*.) From the wide-open rooftop restaurants, the sounds of the Muslim prayer-calls provided a meditative soundscape to the ethereal visuals of lake and palaces.

The sounds in Udaipur and, later, Pushkar, are not all meditative, however. Man, Rajasthan is a noisy place! I miss the quiet nights in the south, where I could actually sleep undisturbed by the sounds of the street. Ironically, Palolem, Goa, known to some as a party beach, has a noise bylaw that restricts noise at night. But in these lovely northern towns, there's always at least a few wedding celebratory parades at all hours of day and night. These are long processions headed by brass bands with snare drums, the musicians in identical, western-style band uniforms and colourful turbans, and behind them are children dancing, women in beautiful *sari* finery, happy, hooting men swinging lanterns and pumping their fists in the air and a decorated cow/elephant/camel or two. The bride and groom sit in a garishly lit-up carriage in the middle of it all. And then the sky is filled with the thundering fireworks. Over and over again. Yeah. The first few times, it's exciting – oooh, a parade! But after a while . . . . We also missed the varied food in Goa – it's "veg" here, even "pure veg," which means no eggs, though, interestingly, yogurt and milk are allowed.

After Udaipur, we rode what must have been the milk-run day bus to the sacred Hindu city of Pushkar and were squeezed in our seats by all kinds of locals carrying all kinds of parcels and decrepit suitcases, while the bus made many stops that added three hours on our supposedly six-hour journey. But we enjoyed watching the Rajasthani landscape unfold before us, including a ten-kilometre stretch of places that sell marble, with names like "Best Marbles." Lining the highway are endless stacks of huge white slabs of the famed non-porous, glittery marble that the Taj Mahal is made of, and trucks roll past carrying small mountains of the hard white stuff.

Pushkar was much bigger and busier than the guidebook had us imagining. Although a sacred site like Hampi (no meat, eggs or alcohol), it's not as peaceful. Its holy lake, where pilgrims come to bathe and important leaders like Gandhi get their bodies' ashes dumped, is dry now due to a recent lack of monsoons in the north. (Yes, climate change is starkly apparent here: no monsoons in the north mean dry riverbeds and lakes, while too many monsoons in the south mean flooding. And then there are the cyclones.) We enjoyed walking along the *ghats* surrounding the dry lake, doing our own version of

"Pushkar *puja*," and visiting India's only Brahma temple. Adam, as usual, made friends with locals his age who called him "brother," and thus I was their "second mother."

The boys here fly small square-shaped kites from the flat rooftops, skillfully controlling them by running the strings through their fingers and stretching their arms out this way and that. From a distance, and if you didn't know (like I didn't at first), you'd think these boys were dancing on the rooftops. There's a big kite festival and flying competition in January or February, and everyone looks forward to it. The trees in Pushkar are filled with little kite carcasses.

We also went on an overnight camel trek in the desert. I had a guide sitting behind me, sharing the saddle and guiding my camel, Krishna, but Adam chose to ride alone on his camel, Shakti. We rode for a few bumpy hours to a hut where Adam and I and our trekking companion, a sweet American named Michelle, were treated to a home-cooked meal. We all sat on the tiny kitchen floor while two women squatted by the stoves and cooked us *daal* and rice and *aloo gobi* and *chapati*, all the while sharing cooking tips and stories from their lives. It was a wonderful, intimate experience, and, after a little bonfire of twigs outside, we went to bed with warm, full feelings.

Then the wedding celebration began. Yes, even way out in the desert, in (as we saw the next day) hundreds of tents and makeshift structures. Apparently, a rich army colonel was marrying off his son to the tune of what would equal a few hundred thousand Canadian dollars. And there were tunes indeed. Loud music blasting until 5:00 AM. I was kept awake, encouraged occasionally by the DJ yelling "Good night!" then disappointed when yet another song blared. Not a peaceful sleep in the desert.

Now we're in Agra, and we saw the Taj Mahal today. We recognized the marble from our bus trip. Its splendour is fading due to pollution, and the river behind it is dry. But it's still magnificent. The rest of Agra is crappy – the most dirty, dilapidated city we've seen. Adam finds irony in the world-renowned, perfect, pristine beauty of the Taj in the midst of the sheer ugliness and filth of the city.

We lingered in the grounds for hours, gazing at the Taj and engaging in philosophical debate about the big issues: truth, beauty, happiness, reality. Everyone in India is a philosopher, and no wonder. Something about being here brings one right to the important stuff. If countries have characters or represent aspects of ourselves, are we drawn to those places that correspond to what we need to explore *in ourselves*? Or are we drawn to those places, those countries, because we already know that part of ourselves so well that going there is like coming home? India has lived in me a long time, but it took me most of my life to get here.

Subject: Night Train to Varanasi

From: Lauren Van Mullem

I swung the heavy duffel bag over my shoulder, feeling it dig into my skin, and tightened my grip on my big, brown, stained travel purse, careful not to press my finger down on the rivet that sticks up like a tack on the strap. I found that defect in London a few summers ago and never bothered to file the point down, figuring that any purse-snatcher would have a deservedly unpleasant experience if he tried to take this bag. Now avoiding the sharp bit of metal has become second nature, and I think of it as a little joke between the two of us.

My tour group of fifty- to sixty-year-old ladies collected their bags from the back of the tour bus in the dirt parking lot of the Delhi train station, waving away would-be helpers eager to haul our luggage for a few rupees. We didn't need help, even if in order to reach our train we had to climb stairs and ramps and dodge more people than there are at Disneyland on a Saturday in July.

In early evening, the Delhi sky turns lavender above floating dust that never seems to settle. The dust covers everything and smells like shit, but in a not-unpleasant barnyard way that makes me think of the country town where I grew up. I had to concentrate to follow our Delhi guide through the crowds while checking on Nissa, the oldest member of our tour at seventy-five years, every few seconds to make sure she was okay. We wove through people, waited, climbed stairs and ramps, waited, shuffled down again and finally reached our train car.

The train from Delhi to Varanasi is a twelve-hour overnight trip. The nicest cars have narrow bunk beds, four to a compartment, curtained off from the main hallway. Because of the size of our group and the general inability to make plans in India, we couldn't all fit in contiguous compartments, and some of the ladies were adamantly against mingling with "the foreigners." Our leader, Beth, diplomatically handed out seating assignments that were amenable to everybody and asked me if I would be comfortable in a compartment with an Indian family. She said I seemed to be "adventurous," a compliment of which I very much wanted to prove myself worthy, since I didn't see myself that way.

Before 9:00 PM, travellers on the night train sit on the lower bunks to talk to one another and drink *chai* from paper cups. The other three bunks in my section were occupied by a mother dressed in a *sari* and bangles; a father, a man with a bright, intelligent face and friendly though inquisitive eyes; and a very well-behaved little boy playing on a hand-held game and asking his mother questions in English and Hindi. I sat down on the lower bunk with my journal, jotting down notes and filling in the blanks of the last two days when the father asked me where I was from, what I did and how far I got in school. I responded and immediately felt that my lack of a Master's degree disappointed my audience. I told him that I was a writer, though I was only just starting to feel comfortable with that declaration, and he perked up. "My wife is a journalist in Hindi," he told me. The mother joined the conversation at that moment and told me that she was a journalist covering current affairs and health for a Hindi publication, and their son was an anchor-boy for a children's news program. The father was a Humanities professor at a local university, and Varanasi was their home.

I asked them to tell me about Varanasi, which the professor father was only too qualified to do, in great detail. He told me that it's one of the holiest Hindu cities, full of art and culture. He and his wife also assured me that no one had ever fallen out of the top bunk on a train. I suggested that I might be the first.

I admired the mother's bangle which was swirled in yellow, red, blue and green with reflective diamond-shaped metal chips all the way around. She quickly said "I have plenty," and dug around in her purse, pulling out two more. She insisted that I take one, but it quickly became apparent that my giant western monster-hands would not take a delicate bangle. She insisted that it would go on, and over the next three minutes she moulded, squeezed, massaged and mangled my left hand until the bangle slid over and landed on my wrist (which, thankfully, is thin). There is a technique to putting on bangles and this woman was a master. I accepted the fact that the only way the bangle was ever coming off was if it disintegrated of its own accord. I loved it.

My top bunk was narrow with no railing and felt very high off the ground. I pushed my purse and sandals to the wall and wrapped my legs around the bags, covering them and myself with a brown blanket when it was time to sleep. Thieves walk up and down train hallways during the night, looking to steal belongings from sleeping passengers, so it's best to keep everything tucked as far away from the edge of the bunk as possible. I used the duffel as a pillow and covered my head with one of my newly acquired scarves for extra warmth. Only my nose peeped out.

An hour after lights-out, just when I began to doze, an official in military dress entered the car, checking assignments and paying special attention to foreign travellers. He seemed to already know that this car had white female tourists inside. When he pushed aside our curtain, the Indian mother was upright in a blur of movement and didn't let him get half a sentence out before she started bombarding him with Hindi. In my half-asleep state, I had a vision of a bird defending its nest against a crow. For fifteen minutes she argued and berated, the auditory equivalent of machine gun fire but without pauses to reload. Frustrated, the man left to bother the other passengers, and my defender returned to her bunk under mine.

I have no idea what she said, and she never explained. Even though the entire scene was in Hindi, I got the gist. It was about me, and officials who like to push white women travellers around. And that Indian mother was having none of it.

Subject: At the Travel Agency

From: Sonja Bricker

Dearest Abby,

The dark alleyways twist right, left, left. And with another left I am
already hopelessly lost. I wander down a narrow staircase, slippery
and redolent of sandalwood and rot. The passage is getting darker.
And people are scurrying past me, like waves, and I let myself be
carried along in their wake. Without thought I flow into the street,
still bright at 8:00 PM, still crowded with the rickshaws and tuk-tuks
and bicycles flowing past, around the people like me. And we are all
pushed to the periphery.

Now I smell frying potatoes and popcorn, in little paper cones
smeared in oil and salt. I reach for one, try out a smile. Oh, there's
a cow, the two-fingered leper from yesterday, a man peeing into the
gutter, a one-armed girl tugging on my sleeve. I choose to ignore her,
as if a ghost, instead of yelling "*Chello*" as Bob does. I, too, am trying
to be a bit of a ghost, in my *salwar kameez* and headscarf. I don't feel
ready to participate in this urgency. I have sought relief, the lightness
I want, in another five milligrams of Valium, only two cents a tablet
here. "Take one per day," said the chemist, and I nodded, wondering
how and when and where I would find the stronger doses, the morphine,
which might indeed assist in the levitation.

Oh Abby, Bob is indeed overjoyed to see me, and he's trying to be
a romantic playmate, buying me little gifts, taking photos, coaxing out
the long orgasms that I love. Reunited after the two-month separation,

we've talked for hours like friends I hope, but it's so clear how differently we approach the world, and India. I witness his altercations nearly every hour when some "stupid" Indian needs to be told how he shouldn't be acting a certain way because it's backward. And I leave the scene, again and again, scurry across the street, nauseous and confused. I am still reeling at this country's chaos, not caring how fucked up it is. Because obviously it just is . . . .

But then today I couldn't escape Bob's gaze or anger and had to sit in it, nearly drowning. We were at the travel agency where we went to book three different tickets: Delhi-Varanasi, Allalahbad-Delhi and Delhi-Kathmandu. First, it took two hours to make known all our destinations, dates, prices, etc. Our agent, a beautiful young woman, kept disappearing to the back room then reappearing, but always without having checked one important detail or another, and disappearing again. Eventually she found us flights and prices (I was to be eligible for an advertised youth fare for ages twelve to thirty, twenty-five percent off) and told us they would deliver the tickets to our hotel at 7:30 PM. Bob refused. Our dodgy hotel, this dodgy travel agency with the payment first, of course it sounded like a classic scam. He said we would wait. The beautiful woman said alright, but it will be at least an hour, so why not come back at 5:00 PM?

Satisfied, we set out along the wide, covered marketplace of New Delhi, all marble and circular, very orderly and British, and wandered into a posh little café full of middle-class Indians. We sat amongst them and lost ourselves in food served on half a dozen silver bowls and platters. We didn't speak really, only murmured sighs of delight. By then it was 5:00 PM, and our food was still half-eaten. Bob called the agency and returned red-faced and sweating. Apparently I was not eligible for the youth fare since I was thirty-one, and so our tickets weren't printed.

We left that gorgeous food behind, that calmness, and rushed back to the agency. And the yelling began. It was my country this and your country that and you are a fucking monkey, can't you answer my question how old is she, she's thirty years old, look at the passport, do the math you fucking monkey . . . . On and on he gushed and finally

I stood up: Stop it, stop it, I want to figure this out. It was clearly a problem of semantics – the youth fare is for people ages twelve to twenty-nine, the way we look at age. Once you turn thirty you are not thirty anymore; you are thirty and, in my case, two months.

Bob wanted to storm out, fuming we're not going to Khumba Mela now, we're not going, I'm not going to give you people my business, why didn't you tell us this hours ago, take us away from our meal. I calmly said it was alright, just charge me the full fare, please print the ticket now, it's getting late. And we waited. And waited. And finally the tickets were before us and we walked out, Bob cursing and me shaking, practically falling down the stairs in the darkness.

Back at the hotel Bob was his joyous self again. YEAH! We're going to the Mela, YEAH Varanasi, it's so cool! Fuck yeah, VARANASI! And I began my retreat, thinking about the effects of my actions back at the agency, which I guess provided the necessary balance. But oh, if this continues, these outbursts, it just won't work. I don't want to be the counterbalance. I just want to be the adventurous girlfriend, cruising Rajasthan on the back of his Royal Enfield, soaking it in.

I'm fully tranquilized again, but, what, am I to stay medicated? It's only day three.

Hugs and kisses,

Sonja

MUMBAI

Subject: Just Enough
From: Bronwyn McBride

Somewhere in Mumbai, an elephant waits at the side of the road in the night. Shifting his weight on legs like leathery tree trunks. Dismissed from a wedding party, with nowhere else to go, the elephant man now sits atop the elephant and smokes a *beedi*. Spitting dry smoke into the wet air.

Somewhere in Mumbai, a kindergarten class is wrapping up for the day. Some of the teachers are Muslim women in their early twenties who were married seven years ago.

"*Bada gol banaenge*" they sing before ending the day, sending the children home. The teachers veil their beautiful faces and slip black, embroidered *burqas* over brightly coloured *salwar kameez*. Prepared to head out into a world that is darker than the coloured blocks and cheerful songs of inside.

Somewhere in Mumbai, thousands of people swarm like angry bees on a honeycomb in a local train station. Covered by corrugated metal roof. Above, one lone goat trots across the tin, hooves making small sounds. Baking in the sun.

Somewhere in Mumbai, teen girls wavering between tradition and modernity visit different places of faith on their day off. Looking for something that no one has a name for. They visit a church, a *mandir* and, finally, the Haji Ali Masjid, getting drenched in the downpour on their way. Then they eat *ceetaphal* cream and head home to change clothes. When they come back into the house, Mom greets them at the door with a scolding for getting wet. Momentarily forgetting what she had been doing beforehand.

Somewhere in Mumbai, a thin dog with jutting ribs tries to cross a busy intersection. He is confused, scared of everything from having only known abuse. He darts this way and that to avoid being struck by auto-rickshaws whose drivers hurl out curses with abandon. The dog finally settles in the shade between a tea stall and a cell phone *wallah*. Gazing reproachfully, but hopefully, at all that life has offered him. Not much, but just enough.

Somewhere in Mumbai, a Ukrainian girl is perched like a bird on the bathroom counter in a five-star hotel. Her long legs are folded, feet are in the sink so that she can be close to the mirror. There, she paints her face and pouts her lips to look like the sexy white doll she is being paid to be for some wealthy Indian's party. Another one sleeps, a pile of curves and angles in tight clothes on the edge of a stage. Pumping music surrounds and fills and empties the space.

Somewhere in Mumbai, an unseen and unremarkable little girl carries water in a cracked plastic container on her head. .

"*Paani leke jao*," an uncle had barked. Her careful feet pick around the debris that litters the construction site she's grown up on. Water leaks from the container, sitting in beads in the part of her hair before rolling down her forehead. A drop falls from the tip of her nose onto her bottom lip and she tastes it. If she was in another life, she would have had more things and wouldn't have had to carry water. Maybe she would have gone to dance classes and birthday parties.

A man wakes up in the morning and finds himself paralyzed, unable to move from his bed. He lies there all day wondering and without explanation; what to say to his boss. Sometimes the city is too much.

A girl finally opens herself to a man, only to be disappointed. In front of her now is only all of his body and none of the feelings that she wants.

A baby turns over in the night, away from his mother's sleeping figure. He wakes up wailing and lost until she takes him close to herself and her old clothes. Offering everything she has: not much, but just enough.

Subject: The Arrival

From: Renée Sarojini Saklikar

The flight was as expected: bad food, cramped seats. I should have gone Toronto-London; my arms and legs, pretzels, all doughy with ache from the Vancouver-Hong Kong-Bangkok-Mumbai route. I've been here only one weekend but already the days elongate. India does that, bends and distorts time.

⌒

Bombay/Mumbai: The night comes down fast, "like a murderer's sweaty palm" (not sure who said that). India assails me with her smell: diesel, dung, an acrid heaviness in the air. (As soon as I set down the word "dung," the spectre of Salman Rushdie rises up, and behind him, all the hundreds of novels, stories, sagas, tales about India and its cities, about this city and its fourteen million inhabitants.) Mumbai dazzles, tires with her sights: on the streets outside this guest house, men in *dhotis* – how does white cotton remain so crisp? Women, sleek with oiled heads, walk in groups of three or four, their bodies wrapped in *saris*, magenta, orange, royal blue. Everyone with necks bent to their palms, carrying hand-held digital devices.

To write about India is to step into a literary eco-system, a habitat of other people's perceptions. Where to begin? Even before a phrase forms, the act of formulation fades, worn and inadequate. I am writing this on my laptop – yes, even in this crumbling Methodist Guest House, there's a wireless connection. This city is both a super-modern metropolis and an anachronism. Outside the walls of the guest house compound, two living streams flow: thousands of words, chatter, smells, colours, everything jumbled, fast, digital; and underneath that layer of bustling activity, the other ageless, timeless India, its dust, dung, cows, the ring of the temple bell at evening, crows and their raucous, mocking calls, ushering night.

Night, at the Chhatrapati Shivaji Airport

This renovated airport is huge: smooth concrete, glass, polished surfaces; its architecture announces, See the new India! But in each corner there exists, of course, the old India: peddlers, hawkers, beggars, dirt, dust, dung (these latter, the three "D's" of India).

Everything's changed since last time I was here; everything's confusing. My jaw clenches, releases. Will Uncle have orchestrated a "special arrangement" with the customs officials? Yes. I'm plucked from our line-up by a woman who calls out my Indian name, "Saroj, Saroj." I approach the woman, and she points to a small man with blood-shot eyes. He holds an old high school grad photo, from Mississauga: there I am – long hair, geeky glasses, a studious expression, good Indo-Canadian girl. I resist the urge to snatch the photo out of the man's hands.

"Did my uncle send you?"

The man nods his head in a circular manner, asks to see my passport, eyes flicking from passport to grad photo, back and forth. His lips settle into a line and again his head moves in that classic Indian gesture, first one way, then the other, not quite yes, not quite no. And I realize this is Uncle's peon, showing me the way to the luggage. At the luggage depot, Uncle's peon consults with two men, uniformed officials. The sweat under my arms collects. I'm an Indo-Canadian, speaker of English, with only a smattering of Hindi and Gujarati, on a study tour of India, my birthplace. I've nothing to fear. I watch Uncle's man in deep discussion with the men dressed in khaki. And then he appears: my uncle, in suit pants, a dazzling white shirt, open at the neck.

Uncle speaks to a Mumbai customs officer, a tall man, well over six feet, hair thinning at the crown of his head, brown skin light as café au lait. Uncle is shorter, chunkier, distinguished by a high forehead, full lips.

He speaks a cadence rarely heard now in Mumbai – a kind of Bombay-English, more formal than "Hinglish," still sing-song, but not as "Mum-baiyya."

Uncle: "Sir, we'll be taking my niece if everything is in order."

Customs officer: "Quite right."

Both men hold me under their gaze. Eyes downcast, my face shape-shifts into the imagined visage of a good Indian girl, not a thirty-year-old international adventurer. Uncle swivels his head in a once-yes-once-no circular motion, much in the same manner as his peon (still nameless, sent by Uncle, palm extended towards the uniformed officials who hover at our side). The customs officer, smiling, nods twice and the officials move away.

And so we set off for Vile Parle (east) and my father's family home, Shanti Doot, "House of Peace," in my uncle's Ambassador, upgraded, he says, to run "smooth, just like Mercedes." The car purrs comfortably and oh, I am that glad to be in it and not out there, on the streets of Mumbai. The night journey from the airport to Vile Parle, where my family has lived for two generations, telescopes time: the night, inky black, lit by street lights and dung fires, shows glimpses of filth, sleeping beggars on streets, rusted iron cans glowing orange, garbage piled, tottering against the cans, side-by-side with racks of bicycles, dust stirred and sifting through the haze of the city at night. Men in groups cross and re-cross street corners, wait at intersections, their legs poke out of white *dhotis*; young men in open-necked shirts and suit pants, everyone with their cell phones. Taxis honk, street peddlers call out *Chaat, Chaat, limbu paani, limbu paani, first class Sony, first class Sony* .... My palms sweat in the air-conditioned comfort of my uncle's car.

Night, at Shanti Doot, with my family

Uncle boasts of the renovations to Shanti Doot: he's installed an elevator for its four stories. In Grandma's garden, the roses bloom in raised beds. When my aunt and cousins greet me, I remember to drop to my knees, briefly, forehead to the floor in an age-old Hindu pantomime: obeisance to elders, the body as a mechanism for honour.

But my bow, such as it is, envelopes everyone in awkwardness and after only a few seconds genuflecting, two large Dobermans bound up and lick my face. Uncle hails them, "Alfred-bhai and Jessie-Princess," a typical family mish-mash, we of the never-never Bombay-Bollywood Raj, a made-up set of affectations laced with pet names for family and equally ludicrous names for the pets themselves. Auntie scolds Uncle about the dogs, who run, slobbering, away. She claps her hands and calls for Cook, old Mustafa, whom Uncle always calls Muss.

With a circular head-nod from Uncle, Mustafa stoops to my suitcase. Another programmed ritual: the long absent daughter of the eldest son, finally returning to her roots, will now eat a late-night meal. Of course I gush thanks. Also, inside, a kind of fear clamps my insides. Everything familiar, yet everything so strange. Part of me wants to instantly materialize back home in Vancouver. My stomach heaves at the thought of having to stay. But I settle in, unpack, and eat *roti*, *daal*, rice with warm *ghee*. Auntie's cook places everything before me with a little sigh. Once I've finished, the great gift-giving ceremony begins. I can't help but sense disappointment. Auntie, Uncle, my cousin-sisters and cousin-brother stand and watch me unpack and hand over books, T-shirts, wee bits of Canadiana trinkets. Why did I choose these? Squatting over my opened suitcase, I catch a glimpse of my cousin-brother looking down, texting his business associates.

Under a mosquito net. In my room, where my grandma and great-grandma once slept. The house of my grandfather, the high court judge; where my father brought my mother, the new daughter-in-law, disowned from her family, a Muslim girl marrying a Hindu boy. Did she lie here and think, as I did, why have we come to this place? *What have we done?* echoes around my bed. Sweat glazes my upper lip. The white muslin of the mosquito net sways infinitesimally under the force of the air conditioner. I sneeze from that mixture of chill and humid, dust and tiredness, known to all who travel through climate zones, cold to hot, the hot chilled artificially.

From Vile Parle to Bombay Central

It takes us well over an hour from Vile Parle (east) to the Methodist Guest House. Driver absent, reason unknown, Uncle expertly weaves

in and out of people, cows, bicycles, construction – everywhere
super-condos, cranes, work crews imported from Sri Lanka, even
Afghanistan, Vietnam. The car is clean, comfortable. But outside:
filth, rags, people, people – a man squats in a gutter to relieve
himself. Inside me, a kind of panic: all diseases lurk here, my blood
seems to sing to me, in the wan trees and narrow side streets, but
most of all in the people, who stare, stare. Even though sealed in the
air-conditioned comfort of the car, that "India-Mumbai" smell seeps
in: feces, diesel, dust, moisture. The streetscapes burst high-rises, and
below them, that other India, the one that never goes away.
Everything is contrast: the gleam of new concrete and steel
structures; and at ground level, families eat, drink, cook, shit, wash
– it's a cycle of life. In me: pride at the strength of these people (my
people?) for surviving. And also, that other part of me (is it North
American?). All I think of is *dirt, disease* – how can I stay clean? How
can I avoid all of it out there? Am I ashamed to write this or just in a
state of disbelief? What is this place? Who am I?

We stop by my cousin-brother's office tower and get out of the car,
parked by a valet. Through glass and concrete we enter the world of
New India. Everything gleams of marble, the air so chill I shiver as
we walk by potted plants, orchids, a fountain of running water, grey
slate, smooth oval stones, up a sleek elevator to the twenty-fifth floor,
LCD screens on the wall, CNN-India. In my cousin's office, laptops,
a wall-mounted flat screen TV. Cousin waves us in. Of course he's on
the phone, a small device tucked into his ear. I stand and look down
at the street, far, far below.

Morning at the Methodist Guest House

The old Methodist Guest House is "dirty, dusty, *sub-standard*," Uncle
pronounced when he dropped me off. I won't see my family now for
two weeks. Tomorrow I join a Canadian International Development
Agency (CIDA) for a study tour of Bangalore, but first we'll take a
trip out to the Dharavi slum. What will happen when image meets
reality? In my mind, stored up and saved: the complexity of Mumbai/
Bombay rendered in pictures from *Slumdog Millionaire*, online photos,
instantly available, posted by "eco-tourists" like me, everyone now a

documentarian. And this place, India, a subcontinent striated with endless variation: language, dialect, region and religion, history, each of its over one billion inhabitants with their own story.

I'm starting to relax in this funny anachronism of a guest house with faint twinges of the Raj. At tea time, the tea is laid out by a server in what Uncle would call "*mufti*" – red oversized turban, white cotton tunic and narrow leggings, curved-toe red leather slippers. My cousins would snort and say, "Hollywood/Bollywood," and turn to their digital devices. I ask the server's name and he bows at me, winks (!) and says, "John, from Mangalore, ma'am." In the courtyard, in the centre of the three-story structure, are potted palms, a few moth-eaten ferns, dingy rattan chairs, rickety bamboo tables. I love it. Best of all, this place is quiet, walled away from Out There – and, look, on a book shelf, *The Norton Reader of English Literature*. What succour. Somewhere, very faintly, the sound of a violin.

I look up to blue sky framed by layers of balconies, all the guest rooms built to open out into this courtyard. I hold the *Norton Reader* in my hands. Sunlight filters down, the heat of the day just starting to rise up from the terracotta stone.

Subject: Monsoon Rain

From: Bronwyn McBride

Even before it rains, water hangs in the air. The wind starts to blow, warm and persuasive. Palms are flattered: they dip and lower their heads. Long grasses blush and look the other way.

Women scramble to manage their fluttering *dupattas*. As the sky darkens and the air thickens, they tuck their phones into their purses and slip their purses into plastic bags. Micro-managing moms pull raincoats over their school-going kids at the first drop. Water bottles held by straps bump against kids' chests. White socks slide down their little ankles as they slog onwards, humpbacked because of their backpacks under their coats.

Rickshaw *wallahs* know they're everyone's last hope and become pompous with attitude.

"They won't take you anywhere!" fumes an Auntie, who has been waiting outside the general store with three grocery bags for half an hour. Her plastic-bagged purse is wet. Her groceries are wet. She is wet, and the fight is over. What to do? The river of rain rushes down from a higher road and creates a creek in which she stands, waiting.

Outside the train stations, traffic slows to a stop and people weave between parked cars, holding newspapers and shawls uselessly over their heads. People and animals and vehicles fill every inch of available space. Truck drivers turn off their engines and put their feet up, examining the bunions on the sides. Taxi *wallahs* spit *paan* saliva out the window into the water that spills over the ground. A drop of red into a brown river.

Thin and wiry men surrender almost completely to the weather, except for the inverted plastic bags on their heads, like chef caps. They walk unhurriedly, letting warm rain soak their faded clothes. Begging kids have no qualms about getting wet, as no one expects any maintenance of appearance from them. They point their faces up while everyone else points theirs down. They choose to dance, pumping skinny arms into the watery air.

Subject: Sharukh Kahn and I

From: Janis Harper

Mumbai is the usual vibrant chaos, maddening and wonderful, and I'd never before seen Adam speechless like he was in the taxi from the airport to the hotel. For a talkative sixteen-year-old, this was way out of character. And the best example of culture shock that I've ever witnessed!

Near the hotel district, on the tourist-crowded Colaba Causeway, I was, surprisingly, remembered from last year by some of the cool, young and oh-so-masculine touts in fedora hats. Apparently all of the sidewalk selling and begging is organized and run by a large gangster group, just like in *Slumdog Millionaire*. But to us unsuspecting tourists, it looks as muddled as everything else. These dudes harass everyone walking down the shop-stall crowded sidewalks to buy-buy-buy, but when you stop to really talk to them, you find out they're sweet, gentle people.

Indians switch roles easily; it's as if we're all supposed to know we're in this crazy improvised play together. And each of us takes whatever role is appropriate at the time. More than once, in the midst of an intense bargaining session with an obstinate tout, I've had to turn my head away for a second to fall out of character and release a pent-up smile, before getting back to the serious role-playing required.

Our first full day in India, we were extras in a Bollywood commercial. I ran into the same casting agent guy I met last year who roams Colaba, trawling for foreign extras for movies and TV. You get an experience in a real Bollywood studio and five hundred rupees, plus food, a day. Some travellers manage to extend their travels – or even live here – doing this kind of work. Our commercial was for the latest Hyundai, a popular car in India.

After a long bus ride to the studio on the outskirts of Mumbai, with a dozen fresh, young, white backpackers, we were all dressed in Victorian period costume and had our hair shellacked in place and makeup layered on. Adam got long fake sideburns, and I got a tall updo. The dressers kept misjudging my size, and I spent way too long sweating profusely in a hot, tiny closet of a makeshift dressing room, feeling there was something wrong with my body, trying to squeeze in and out of heavy gowns, while not ripping them or soaking them with my sweat. The other women were already dressed and coolly chatting with each other, looking splendid, while I laboured clumsily away.

The final dress possibility almost fit but not quite, so some Indian guy had to sew it together at the small of my back while I was still in it. Although the situation was certainly strange, the people seemed professional, so I had surprisingly few misgivings about standing half-dressed among a bunch of Indian men, and letting one of them put their hands down my backside with a needle and thread. The upper back of the beautiful dress, unable to be zipped up, remained open during the shoot, exposing my bra and bare back. I felt a bit vulnerable.

The buzz was that we were going to be in a TV commercial with Sharukh Khan himself. There weren't a lot of us – maybe thirty extras altogether – and after we'd been positioned and repositioned by the director, and given direction and several rehearsal takes, the man himself walked in. The few Indian extras on set tried to restrain themselves, but I heard them whisper, awestruck, behind me, "There he is! That's Sharukh Khan!"

Sharukh Khan is a hunk. And a very talented actor, dancer and singer. A brand unto himself, he is the most ubiquitous star in India, and although he's in his forties, is lusted after by women of all ages and admired by men. All good reasons to be called "The King of Bollywood." Add to that his popularity around the globe (yes, even in distant North America), and you can see why he's also called by some, "the world's most famous movie star." And he seemed like a really nice guy! Pleasant, polite and humble. Of course, being the consummate professional, it wasn't necessary for him to do many takes – and between each one, he smoked as many cigarettes as he possibly could – so his day was much shorter than ours.

The director liked what I was doing so much that she put me in the vicinity of the King, so I'm quite visible, with my hair piled high on my head, in a shiny green gown, waving a fan and getting exasperated at the end – because the great star screwed up his lines yet again. *That Sharukh!* The scene of the commercial is a production set of a movie, with the actors (and extras) playing movie actors and directors working on a scene that is set in Victorian England. Sharukh plays himself, only he's distracted because he's daydreaming about the i10 Hyundai rather than the love interest who, unfortunately, has a similar name, Irene. It's sophisticated and post-modern – and, in its playing around with time periods and multiple roles, also very Indian. I know what the final product looks like because, not long after, we'd see our commercial over and over on our hotel TV in Goa. I was thrilled at first – seeing myself on TV in India, of all places! – though eventually I stopped watching, it was on so much. Ho hum. But what a great ad. Edited beautifully, it's slick and funny and clever. And the YouTube comments on the "i10 Hyundai Dreams" TV commercial gush with love and adoration for the handsome Sharukh.

Back in Mumbai, after our brush with the King of Bollywood, I notice that Adam has quickly become acclimatized: he's already learned how to cross the streets amid the dangerous mayhem of honking traffic (a practice I'm still not very skilled at) and how to bargain hard. We dined that night on egg *biryani* in Leopold's Café – the restaurant made famous by *Shantaram* author Gregory David Roberts. In the glass of our table were bullet holes from last year's terrorist attacks.

En route

Subject: The Girl in the Grey Dress
From: K. Lorraine Kiidumae

It was a hot and sunny Sunday afternoon, on January 25, 2009, just two months after the "Mumbai Attacks." On the bumpy ride from the Chhatrapati Shivaji Airport to the Novotel Mumbai Hotel, the air was pungent with the smell of smouldering rubber from the constant burning of rubbish. The bus took a journey past mile after mile of abandoned, dilapidated, old concrete buildings with children dangling from the empty window ledges. Hundreds of people were crowded in the streets, many with bare feet, and laundry hung everywhere. There was the constant honking of horns as the bus driver manoeuvred amongst street sellers hustling their wares, maimed beggars, cows, tractors, bicycles, motorcyclists, rickshaws and automobiles.

Halfway to the hotel the bus passed a giant billboard that spilled out humbling and unexpected optimism: "The Most Worthless Emotion is Self Pity." Not the type of advertising you would see on a billboard in Canada. As I repeated the words over and over again to myself – "The Most Worthless Emotion is Self Pity" – and thought about everything I had just seen, I shrank a little in shame and had to look away.

I thought about the woman I had spoken with the night before at Heathrow Airport, en route to Mumbai. She was from Oxford and was returning home from visiting her fourteen-month-old grandson, Charlie. She started to cry when she told me about leaving him. The *Bhagavad Gita* says you should become one with the Universe and be attached and connected to everyone, not just one person or your family. This is how I find myself starting to feel, since coming to India. On the flight from London to Mumbai, I felt as though I blended right in with the Indians, as though I was somehow connected.

A week later I am sitting in the lounge area at Hodka, in the Kutch Desert, state of Gujurat, with three cushions, a quilt, a little Indian table, an old-fashioned bottle of Coca-Cola and a bottle of water. There are too many people talking around me, but now I don't want to move. I'm one of twenty ladies on the Maiwa Textiles Tour, at a village resort that was developed by the Government of India as a refuge after the earthquake in 2001. Kutch is in the extreme west of India and feels like the "wild west" in a Clint Eastwood movie. And yet, I can see that our tour guide, Amit, sitting at a table in front of me with his laptop, out here in the middle of nowhere, has managed to find an internet connection so he can communicate with his family back home.

We are twenty middle-aged women, miles out in the desert, sleeping in open mud huts under a thatched roof, on beds crafted from mud. We are apparently only twenty kilometres from the Pakistani border, but I have no concept of that and decide it is likely best not to mention it when I email back home.

Other than the smell of burning rubber when I got off the plane in Mumbai, there have been none of the pungent smells that I had been warned about. I have hardly thought of home and have not felt homesick, except for our little house on the water in Nanoose Bay, thoughts of which I wake up with every morning and fall asleep with every night.

Yesterday I looked in the mirror and felt like Kathleen, like myself, like the way I think my mother thinks of me. When I feel earthy, kind, natural, likeable, with my hair curly from the morning dew, at peace, uncomplicated and open. I have felt that way a lot on this trip, and I like it. In fact, I have felt so at home in India, it is as though I belong here, or came from here and have come back. I could travel alone here I feel so comfortable.

I have taken over three hundred and fifty photographs already. Every other moment is a picture. There is a synchronicity to everything. With the flow of the bicycles, pedestrians, cows, goats, bulls, camels and rickshaws, weaving back and forth, it is as if the pattern of life is being embroidered in time, in this moment, like the movement of the looms and needles and trestles creating crafts.

Today we watched a bell maker sculpt a brass bell from beginning to end. I bought a xylophone from him for five thousand rupees, about one hundred and fifty dollars. It is made of seven brass bells in ascending sizes and set in a hammered brass box. It was his masterpiece, and he had won an award for his work. I almost felt guilty, like I was stealing it from him, until our tour guide told me that, for him, five thousand rupees was equivalent to five thousand Canadian dollars, and very few people earn that much in a month.

The bell maker seemed honoured that I bought the xylophone. He had his son carry it for me. The whole village accompanied us, along with the rest of our tour group, as we ambled in procession back down the narrow, dusty road to the bus. Even though we had already been given tea upon arrival, to show his gratitude, the bell maker's son insisted on boarding the bus with a fresh pot of hot *masala chai* and served it to us in chipped saucers. They did not have enough cups. It was one of my best moments of the trip.

The children here follow us to the bus, and chase after us, asking us to take their photographs and then squealing with delight when we show them their images on the screen of the camera. It's like going a hundred years back in time. Canada seems so bland, big, cold, affluent, wasteful, excessive, greedy and so far from real life it is an almost unimaginable comparison. Life in India is simple yet exciting, warm and lively, with people everywhere dressed in their colourful *saris* or *kurtas* and turbans, even when hanging laundry or working in the fields.

In one of the travel books I have about India there is a line that says, "Anyone who goes to India once will always return." A *jyotishi* would say instead, "If there is anyone who has visited India and India wants them to return, she will call them back again." Although I have not even left yet, I am already hoping she will call me back.

We are now down to the last week of our trip and are en route to Bappa's, the owner of Bai Lou Studio, in Kolkata. The flight from Delhi had been delayed, although for what reason remains a mystery. I sensed there was something we weren't being told, because men in army fatigues stood with rifles pointing straight out, ready to shoot. Piles of luggage were removed from the plane and heaped onto the tarmac in the hot sun, then reloaded two hours later so the flight could take off. The airline crew chattered continuously and excitedly in Hindi back and forth to each other, while smiling reassuringly at the passengers. But somehow I felt they might have been laughing at us a little, in a good-natured way, for managing to pull the wool over our eyes so easily. However, no attempt at an explanation was given, and I felt apprehensive until we arrived safely at the Oberoi Grand Hotel in Kolkata.

A hurried reshuffling of plans and itinerary was made by cell phone, and we had only a few minutes to throw our luggage into the room, freshen up and get back onto the bus that brought us from the airport. It is rush hour in Kolkata, and the bus idles in the hottest part of the day, stuck amidst some construction, while the air conditioner cools twenty middle-aged ladies from Canada.

Helen and I have been sitting in companionable silence for the last fifteen or twenty minutes, while the bus rolls and bobs up and down over the broken pieces of concrete that used to be the road. We had been appointed as roommates for the India tour and, for the most part, have been quite suited to one another. By now Helen has become accustomed to my habit of spreading the contents of my suitcase all over our hotel room the minute after we arrive, while her things are neatly piled and organized inside her own suitcase. And, formerly a non-drinker, she now seems to rather enjoy joining me in a glass (or two or three) of wine, which I must have at the end of each day, regardless of what time it is. And, for my part, I am no longer alarmed by Helen's habit of talking to herself while going about her routines, such as brushing her teeth or packing her suitcase. As I'm falling asleep, I anticipate the sound of her false teeth clinking as they touch the bottom of the glass on the nightstand of whatever hotel we are staying in. And I am now familiar with the sound of her breathing, and the occasional nasal moaning, as Helen sleeps, otherwise soundlessly, on her back.

The bus has stopped at a red light. Helen and I have resumed a previous conversation about the feud going on in her family over her wealthy father's estate. One of her sisters wants all twelve of the demitasse sets that her parents had collected over the years. Helen was saying how her sister was starting to come around and was negotiating a swap for three of the coveted demitasse sets in exchange for some plates from her mother's Lenox Rose china set.

I feel a presence out the window and suddenly become aware of a girl standing on the street corner. Something about her look and the cut of her hair reminds me of myself at her age, which I guess to be about twelve, so I smile at her, but she doesn't notice me. She is wearing a grey dress that isn't buttoned up fully in the back and looks several sizes too big for her. As is the fashion in India, the grey dress hangs over top of a skirt, this one with a pink-green-white checkered pattern. Both the dress and the skirt look well worn. I wonder what she is doing there. She looks up and sees me watching her and smiles, then ducks under a makeshift tent. I feel disappointed that she has left and hope I haven't been rude in staring, but when she comes back out I can see that she has combed her hair for me and slipped a pair of thongs onto her previously bare feet.

There is an older man crouched on the ground next to her, and a pile of pots is attached to a cord and tied to the fence behind them. I realize he must be her father and that they must live there. I am overtaken with emotion, but it isn't pity; it is some sort of a profound inner reckoning of the reality of her situation. All this time I never take my eyes off the little girl in the grey dress, and she smiles again, and then excitedly comes right up to the window next to me and puts her hand to the glass, as if to touch my face. Deeply moved, I smile at her and raise my hand to the glass to reciprocate a touch to her face.

Just then the bus begins slowly lurching bumpily forward through the chunks of dug-up concrete. As I look back at her, tears well up in my eyes to think that she has so little, and yet can find joy in a comparatively affluent older woman having paid her some attention. I have taken several photographs of her, and decide that when I get home, I will have one blown up to look at, and remind myself of how fortunate I am and how little it had taken to bring joy to the girl in the grey dress.

For the rest of my stay in India and for weeks afterward I cannot stop thinking about her; she has touched me in a way I have never felt before. I have told all of my family and friends and co-workers and anyone else who will listen about the little girl in the grey dress. But when I get home and put her photograph up on my computer screen, it makes me feel sad, and I have to take it back down.

Several months go by, and I continue to be haunted by the girl in the grey dress. I contact Bappa to see if he can find her for me from the photograph, so that I can help get her off the street, to send her to school. But Bappa recommends against it.

"If other Indians find out, they will think that all they have to do is smile and approach Westerners and they will be helped. Word will spread, and more Indians will start harassing visitors to the country. Besides," he says, "even if you do it, there is no way to guarantee that her father will use the money for her. And, if he does, she will no longer have a place, for she will not fit in with her family, and she will not fit in with the children whose parents can afford to send them to school."

I ponder all of this for a long time. Here, as a Westerner, I want to help, but Bappa is right, the girl in the grey dress does have a home, and a family and a place. And she does not seem to be overcome by the worthless emotion of self-pity that I had read about on the billboard in Mumbai.

"Am I demeaning her with my own worthless emotions, by bestowing my own sense of values onto her?" I ask myself. But I still can't shake the feeling that my moment with her was tied to the beginning of a destiny I have yet to find. I need to believe that there was a point to all of this and a reason why I can't forget her.

I thought of her smile, of the moment our eyes met, and wondered if by looking at her I had possibly some kind of effect on her life. I, in that same moment, was altered forever, in appreciation of my own life and in a newfound empathy towards other people. Maybe it was only meant to be just that: in that one moment, we found a place of grace.

Subject: A New Notebook
From: Morelle Smith

When we arrived in Delhi, the city was wrapped in freezing fog.
There were people sleeping in the train station, bodies stretched
out, some covered with thin blankets, some with no covering at all.
Men, women and children, close together to keep warm, oblivious
to the people moving around them or stepping over them. Crowds
of people with faces sunk in waiting. Some sitting on bedrolls, some
squatting beside them. It was unbelievably cold.

I had three travelling companions, two English, one Australian,
and they were all determined to head south. In these freezing
temperatures it seemed the obvious thing to do.

We made our way from the station to a nearby café. It was still dark,
but morning was not far away. A few people were stirring in the
streets, walking with bowed heads, wrapped in shawls in an attempt
to keep out the freezing mist. Many more people were lying on the
pavement with only thin shawls to cover them. I realized that the ones
in the station were the lucky ones. These people were totally ill-equipped
for the cold. They wore thin *dhotis* and shirts, their feet were shod in
sandals, and the only concession they made to the cold were the shawls
covering their heads and shoulders. Other tea-drinkers in the café were
shivering in the light of the oil lamps and cupping their fingers around
their mugs.

We travelled south to Mumbai. The train was packed. But trains in
India always are. As well as sitting squashed into the seats, people
squatted or lay down in the aisles and stretched out on the luggage

compartments. A vivacious young Indian lady in an orange *sari* expounded on the glories of Mumbai and its superiority to Delhi.

It was still dark when we arrived in Mumbai. The journey from Delhi had taken all the daylight hours and almost all the night ones too. In that time, we had crossed from winter to summer. The last part of the journey passed through miles and miles of shanty towns, makeshift buildings of corrugated tin, an assortment of old tires and cardboard. The train was going slowly at this point, and these huddled heaps of scrap metal and board made up a sea of crowded, massed poverty. I gazed out of the train window at what looked like a scene from another world. When the train finally pulled into the station, it was filled with the usual quota of recumbent figures, this time undisturbed by the cold. Cockroaches scuttled away from the light, to hide in dark corners.

We went from the station to the ferry to get a boat going south to Goa. It was just beginning to get light as we drove through the streets. Streets of tall buildings full of age and history and human habitation, buildings with shutters and balconies and peeling paintwork, pale buildings in the early light, curiously familiar architecture, but familiar from a memory that could hardly be my own, a memory of history, for I had never seen buildings like that before and yet I knew them, as if a personal veneer of memory had been stripped away, revealing a more ancient, impersonal layer.

Passing through the streets of Mumbai was like entering time's attic where it kept its hidden secrets, not concealed deliberately, not inaccessible, but long forgotten. The stairway to the attic was sealed over with dust, but once discovered, its secrets disclosed, you realized it had never tried to hide anything, it had been yourself who had forgotten and yourself who had to make the effort to explore and rediscover it, learn its secrets and make them part of your own journey. Travelling through the Mumbai streets was travelling back in time.

Chapora Village, Goa

Manohar was about twenty years old, and he sailed the ferry from one side of the Chapora River to the other. He had a mass of curly black hair and dark skin. He did not speak any English but his friend, Vinayak, did, and sometimes the three of us would spend time together, walking on the rocky area by the sea, swimming in the warm water or drinking *chai* in one of the little cafés made out of dried palm leaves.

I learned a few words of Konkani, the local language, but it was not enough to converse. Vinayak did the translating between Manohar and me, and later, between me and his mother and sister.

The Chapora River flowed into the sea which was clear and warm, with long golden beaches, backed by towering coconut palms. There were two small village settlements on either side of the river. The people from the villages had an easy, non-intrusive friendliness, with none of the brashness of city-dwellers in Delhi or Mumbai, who think nothing of coming up to you and asking you endless questions. The women who went to the nearby market in Mapusa came over on the ferry, carrying huge baskets of fish. They wore brightly-coloured *saris* and laughed and joked with each other constantly, hands touching other hands, arms, shoulders, hair. Their long black hair was piled on top of their heads and protected from the sun by coloured cloths. Anklets jingled and silver toe-rings gleamed in the sunlight as they walked.

The English couple had stayed in Mumbai so it was just me and John, the Australian, who set up camp on the other side of the river. We bought provisions at Mapusa market and cooked vegetables and rice on a little fire made from dried palm leaves. We also made porridge from a kind of bran flour and sweetened it with lots of brown cane sugar. During a particularly high tide the level of the river rose and seeped into our tent. We decamped the next day to the near side of the river, closer to the village and on higher ground. When John left, heading back to Australia, I stayed on.

One afternoon, returning to my tent I came upon a scene of devastation. The little tent had been ripped apart. There was a long trail of ants heading towards the pan of lentils I'd left uncovered, thinking it was safe inside the tent, and a second trail heading in the other direction, presumably towards their own larder, stashed carefully away somewhere. The few clothes and my rucksack were untouched as were the two books I'd brought with me, Basho's *Narrow Road to the Deep North* and the *Bhagavad Gita*. But there was no trace of the journal I'd kept since I'd left the UK, a thick pad of paper. Then I spied two torn sheets of paper in a corner and smoothed them out carefully. That was all that was left.

When I reported my loss to Vinayak, he commiserated and explained that it was probably some cows that had ripped the tent and eaten the papers. Cows in India are considered sacred and are allowed to wander around as they please, often helping themselves to fruit and vegetables from people's stalls. I had seen stall owners make shooing movements with their hands, but I had never seen anyone lift a finger to the cows.

Vinayak generously invited me to stay at his family's house. With the woven blanket I'd bought in Delhi as a cover, I slept outside on the porch on a thin piece of matting that I rolled up in the morning.

When I left, Vinayak and Manohar came with me to Panaji where I caught the bus to Mumbai to get a train to Delhi and then to Amritsar. There were tears in Vinayak's eyes as we hugged goodbye. Manohar was more reserved and withdrawn. The heat was intense. I could feel sweat trickling down my legs. There were flies, mosquitoes and cockroaches. I thought of the purple onions, the long white radishes, the rice, cooked with *jeera* and *garam masala*, turmeric and our bran porridge specialty. The little fish, freshly caught that day. I'd become quite adept at making fires of dried palm leaves and cooking over them.

On the train from Mumbai to Delhi I was fortunate enough to secure a seat on one of the hard wooden boards. At every station we stopped in, the *chai* sellers ran alongside the carriages shouting and people opened the windows and bought *chai* in little ochre-coloured pots which they later tossed out of the window so that fragments of brick-red clay littered the platform.

At Delhi, I spent what was left of the night in the Ladies Waiting Room, a harassment-free zone. The next day I went on to Amritsar near the border with Pakistan. It was dark by the time I arrived there, and I took a tonga from the station to the Golden Temple where you can stay overnight for only a few rupees. The pony's harness was covered with bells, and the streets of Amritsar were utterly silent, apart from the clop-clop of the pony's hooves and the jingling of the bells. I wrapped my blanket around me as we headed for the Golden Temple, for already I was much further north and there was a chill in the air.

It was February, and in Europe there would still be no sign of spring. But Europe was a long way away. My rucksack was lighter for having discarded a tent, jacket and thick sweater, but I had added two thin cotton shirts, a pair of cotton trousers, a shawl and some pieces of Indian jewellery – as well as a new notebook.

KOLKATA

Subject: Wait Canada

From: Leanne Leduc

When I went to India, I, like many before me, thought I may volunteer in an orphanage or hospital to help out the needy. However, fairly early on I found I was so overwhelmed by the magnitude of poverty that I gave up on that idealistic plan and just simply tried to make it through every day without losing it. India can be a difficult place to travel; there is so much despair, filth and sorrow, it can blind one's view of the true beauty and wonder of it.

I had been backpacking through India for four months, and it was time to go home to Canada. My sister was getting married! I arrived in Kolkata, where I was flying from, three days prior to my flight. I found a small hotel, and each day I would just wander and take in my last few days in crazy and amazing India.

Each time I left and returned to my hotel there was a mother and her child, a little boy, who were begging out front. Each day I smiled and said hello. And they returned my smiles – genuinely, it seemed. There are so many street people in India, especially in the cities, but these two somehow touched me differently. Perhaps it was because of my upcoming departure: I had already shed my "tough travel girl" shell needed for self-preservation. Perhaps it was because I saw them many times, not just on one three-second encounter where I would smile and say sorry then move on and have to forget them or risk a broken heart. Or perhaps, in my final days, I had actually learned to see past the horrors.

On one occasion when I passed them, the little boy asked where I came from. I stopped, held his grubby little hand and told him I was from Canada. We had a short conversation of niceties, and then I was on my way.

On my final night I was packing my backpack for the last time. I had been on the road for nine months total and had gathered a few things needed while I was travelling, but now that I was headed home, they could be let go. I had some multivitamin tablets, a couple of raggedy worn T-shirts and my trusty "bathroom shoes" – a lovely cheap pair of bright orange plastic flip-flops with white flowers. Bathroom shoes are a necessity when travelling in some countries, since often you don't want to have bare feet while showering or going to the toilet in the night for fear of nasty foot infections or vile roach encounters.

After I had packed, I still had the pile of the things I was not taking with me. Instead of chucking them, I decided to give them to the beggar lady and her son. I popped outside and handed her a plastic bag with "the stuff"; she did not open it in front of me but accepted it graciously and with the most beautiful big grin. Her son was not there, and I hoped I would get to see him again before I left the next morning.

I slept my last night in India and woke early, excited to be heading home. After the usual morning tasks I closed up my pack, did the final ticket-passport-room check and headed out to catch a rickshaw to the airport. When I stepped outside, I noticed that the beggar mother and her child were not there.

My heart sank as I looked around and they were nowhere to be seen. But time was ticking, and I had to be going. I started walking to the main street. I had walked about fifty metres when I heard him. At first it did not register, but then the little voice got louder and louder, and I realized that he was yelling at me. And I realized what he was saying: "CANADA ... CANADA ... CANADA, WAIT CANADA!"

I turned around to see the little beggar boy running towards me, as best he could, in my giant size nine orange, flowered bathroom flip-flops. I knelt down into his outstretched arms and caught a big heartfelt hug. His eyes shone, and with the same big grin his mother had, he said "Thank you, Canada!" He then promptly turned and returned to his mother who stood at the end of the street, and smiled. I returned the smile, waved a final goodbye then caught my ride to the airport.

It was a most memorable and special farewell for many reasons, but mainly because it solidified one of the lessons I had decided I was to learn from India. The saying that "one person cannot change the world" is likely true in many cases. It is easy to become overwhelmed, defeated and give up trying. But if instead of trying to fix everything, we each just improve our own small worlds through kindness, to the people we meet and through the things we do, the whole world would undoubtedly be a better place.

Subject: The Gap

From: Leah Sherry

I feel like Britney Spears. There is no such thing as a private moment. Everyone is watching your every move. And when you stand still on the street doing something outrageous – like buying a tea – if you don't get moving after, like, five minutes, you will draw a traffic-stopping crowd. There are more people living in Kolkata than there are people living in all of Canada. I guess that increases the probability of drawing a traffic-stopping crowd. Mathematically speaking.

Canada. The spacious and crisp. Sigh. How I miss you sometimes, from way over here.

Here. I worked my lily-white ass off to get here. Didn't I come here to save the world? And here I am, looking to get saved. Isn't that the classic line? But I suppose I kind of learned what the "go to India to find yourself" fuss was all about. You see, I have fallen in love. The unthinkable thing. But it's true. I feel something here that makes my bones sing. It makes my ugly feel gorgeous. Makes my lost feel home.

I caught a mere glimpse of it last year – in Canada, remember? When that cat I got puked on my rug, and I worried more about the cat than my perfect rug. In that moment I knew I loved that cat – and that, as a result, I would never be the same. My happiness and that cat's happiness were strung up like a marionette. I actually felt a little sad because of that feeling. Like there was me, this cat and this feeling – the three of us now, instead of just the one of us, or even two of us. I wasn't able to live in a vacuum anymore and still look myself in the eye. I knew my life and my movements, and it all had an impact.

And yet, despite my flimsy experiments with learning to love, I got here, to Kolkata, still cynical, suspicious and cold. And I told everyone

I would NOT give money to beggars. And I didn't. Until I sat with them for a while. Over a dirty cup of *chai*.

Cat didn't really prepare me for this.

A few months later – a few months of street-roaming, Bengali-swearing, *chai*-drinking, rice-fisting, *sari*-tying, wide throat-laughing, high-fiving, pant-sewing, train-hopping, river-bathing, hand-wringing, taxi-cabbing, betelnut-spitting, heart-cranking, edge-stretching, and yes, money-giving – I find myself officially kicked in by this love. Puke on my rug? Fuck, these kids could puke on my lap, puke in my bed, puke in my . . . .

What am I saying here? I am less concerned with the puke of it all.

But actually, speaking of puke: I haven't been sick really. Except that one time when I farted, and I shit my pants. Okay, okay, I know. I always get gross when I am nervous.

Look. I don't know how to tell you this.

I wanted to burn my passport and all of my money. I desperately wanted to feel like we were equals. Me and the kids. The street kids. The kids who make their living by hanging out in this tourist ghetto and charming us, the tourists. After the Bollywood song-and-dance of the day, sure, I would pay them for the work they had done. Entertaining me. Enabling my sense of "authentic" travel and "connection with the locals." Sure, that was worth a few bucks. Cripes. Twenty dollars is like a month of local wage. So, fine. I gave them money. Fine.

But I felt like I wanted more. Not the smoke and mirrors, not the tourist ride. I wanted the real thing. I wanted to see where they really lived, what they really did with the money I gave them. (There are constant rumours in the tourist circles of gangs "owning" the kids and taking their earnings, owning their corners and their mothers.)

So I hung out. A lot. From morning til night. Late late into the night. After all the sidewalks got rolled up. And the song-and-dance started to lighten and fade.

And I felt at ease. And so did they.

Money and food were a given. If I was eating, they were eating. If I was seeing a movie, they were seeing a movie. Equals. I was determined to make it so. Living in solidarity with the poor.

But it seems that no matter what I do, I will never be an equal here. I will never sit toe-to-toe. Should that have been obvious? Am I the last to know?

Problem one: The colour of my skin. And what comes with that. I get to move through the city like a celebrity, just because I am white.

Problem two: I get to travel to Kolkata. With a tourist visa. Just because I am Canadian. Problem three: I get to buy whatever I want, whenever I want, just because my dollar is powerful.

Nothing I do can close the gap. I try to take them to "our" restaurants. Access denied. I give them all of my money. They still need more. I want to bring them home. They don't have passports.

So I got mad. And I thought, fine, I will burn my money and my plane ticket home and my passport and that will strike our balance. And we will be equal because we will possess the same thing of nothing.

And then I had this image of myself as a raging mad, barefoot woman in a tie-dyed *sari*, dancing around a small street-side fire with all of her belongings aflame, while everyone watches and points at her. Not in amazement of her puritan ways, but simply because she can have it all back if she wants. Everything she has burned. With a simple phone call. Or an email home.

Which brings me to my next item of business: I might need you to send me a few bucks.

Don't worry, I am not going to marry anyone here.

THE SOUTH

Subject: One Pen

From: Jennifer Zickerman

On a dusty side-road in south India, a decrepit bus wound its way through small villages, past fields of rice paddies and groves of coconut palms. Along the way, it stopped to pick up schoolchildren: two here, four there, three down the road. As the children boarded the bus, they instantly gravitated to me – a stranger, an oddity, a white woman travelling alone.

"Hello Madam. What is your name? What is your country? One pen please?" Younger children copied the elders, voices rising in a sing-song litany, louder with each repetition. As more children got on the bus the crowd increased, each child shouting to outdo the other, working themselves into a frenzy of exuberance far out of proportion to the excitement of the event.

At first I smiled and joked with them, but this only emboldened them. Now I had three children crammed into the seat next to me, with another dozen pushing from behind and others hanging over the back of the seat in front, all of them laughing and shouting, "One pen! One pen, Madam!"

I tried to hide behind my newspaper. Other people on the bus, whom I hoped might come to my rescue, instead cast disapproving looks on the scene. The children's tidy school uniforms belied the chaos they were creating.

The bus stopped to pick up more passengers. Suddenly the children fell silent as a young woman made her way down the aisle between the seats. The tide of children parted; the crush of children in the seat next to mine hurriedly disentangled their limbs and wiggled out of the way; the ones in the seat in front turned around and pretended that they had been looking out of the window. Paying no attention, with great dignity, the woman sat down beside me and twitched her *sari* into smooth drapes.

She smiled at me. "Hello Madam. What is your name? What is your country?" I laughed, told her my name and where I was from and explained that I was laughing because this silent, demure, well-behaved group of children had, moments before, been an unruly, shoving mob hollering the same questions – plus "One pen! One pen, Madam!" – at the top of their lungs.

She cast her eyes over them, and they looked at their feet, overcome with guilt. "I am their schoolteacher," she said, "and I am very disappointed in them." They writhed with shame. "Their parents would be extremely ashamed if they knew they were behaving like beggar-children, especially to a foreign lady. These are not poor children. Their parents can afford to buy them the things they need for school. And they do not need pens – in school, they use slates."

This was not the first time I heard the cry "One pen!" Driving through a village in southern Morocco, a raucous band of boys ran alongside my car yelling: "Un stylo! Un stylo, Madam!" On an island off the coast of Thailand, at an oceanside hut made of bamboo and thatched palm I smiled at a tiny girl who peeked at me from behind her mother's legs. "One pen?" she peeped. Other travellers have told me of similar encounters in the Peruvian Andes and the Mexican jungle, in the slums of Jakarta and the wealthy neighborhoods of Nairobi. On an internet message board, an aid worker in Afghanistan tells of refugee children begging for pens – not food, not money, not toys, but pens.

In post-industrial countries, pens are ubiquitous and quotidian. They litter our purses, our briefcases and the glove compartments in our cars. They rattle around in desk drawers or are stored with their mates in desk-accessory pen cups. We can never find a pen when we need one because they are of so little value that we don't usually notice their existence. We pick them up by the phone and put them down on the kitchen counter; then, while tidying up, we stick them in a drawer. We steal them from bank tellers and loan them to colleagues who forget to give them back and nobody cares very much. Pens are given away in their tens of thousands by real-estate agents, hotels, pharmaceutical companies and dot-com start-ups. We lose them with impunity, with nothing more than momentary regret, if we even notice their loss. We buy more in boxes of twelve or twenty-five or five hundred.

In contrast, in poorer countries, manufactured goods, even cheap, disposable items like pens, have cachet. Where education is a luxury, pens symbolize literacy. Where schoolchildren use slates and their writing is wiped clean and begun anew a dozen times a day, pens symbolize permanence and the expression of the individual. Where poverty limits consumption, pens symbolize status. And the finer the pen, the greater the status.

I spent an afternoon sitting at the desk of a bank manager in a provincial town in the Indian state of Maharashtra. I needed to withdraw money from an overseas account. After being passed through several nervous clerks, I ended up at a massive desk, bare except for a telephone, a reading lamp and, exactly in the centre, a beautiful gold fountain pen with an intricate pattern on the cap.

The man across the desk was all-accommodating, with oiled hair and a high-buttoned white jacket that strained over his belly. With a wave of his hand, tea was brought for us. The bank was Dickensian: dark and dusty, with tottering stacks of fabric-bound ledgers. Tall wooden filing cabinets with creaky drawers delineated paths that led to small clearings where hunched clerks beetled away in an aura of fear and obsequiousness.

The bank manager's job seemed to consist of signing, or refusing to sign, papers brought to him by his minions. A mute *Namaskar* (the Hindu gesture of respect where the head is bowed and the hands meet at the chest as if in prayer) prefaced each request for his attention. Through a hole in the ceiling above the bank manager's desk, a bamboo basket containing papers was lowered on a rope. A face peered down through the hole, watching the bank manager's reaction. Fingertips visible at the edge of the hole showed that the clerk on the upper floor was doing *Namaskar*, just in case his boss happened to look up.

One by one, the bank manager took pages from the basket, leaned back and perused the contents. Sometimes, without taking his eyes off the page, he shook his head in refusal. The face in the hole registered this judgement with the side-to-side bobble of the head that, in India, signifies understanding and agreement. When a page met the bank manager's approval, he placed it on his desk, picked up his fountain pen, ceremoniously unscrewed the cap and then signed the page in an ornate script with a flourish at the end. Then the pen was recapped and placed back in the exact middle of the desk.

In between signing papers, the bank manager complacently surveyed his domain, his hands folded on his belly, looking like a mix of potentate and water buffalo. I was ignored. To show my impatience, I rose from my chair. It was a futile gesture; I couldn't actually leave because my passport had been spirited away into the warren of ledgers and filing cabinets. The bank manager, as if suddenly noticing me, as if I had – most unfortunate! – slipped from his memory, made placating gestures, urging me to sit down again. We smiled insincerely at one another.

I smiled because I wanted my passport back. He smiled because he was enjoying my inconvenience, enjoying showing his subordinates the power he had over me. More tea was ordered. Picking up his pen, stroking it, he engaged me in conversation, with him speaking Hindi sprinkled with bits of English, and me speaking English sprinkled even less liberally with bits of Hindi. The conversation sputtered out in mutual insincerity and incomprehension.

When the bank manager felt he had extracted every possible drop of status from the situation, he gestured and a clerk emerged from the warren bearing my credit card on a brass salver. The bank manager told me, in suddenly much-improved English, that he was very sorry, it was very unfortunate, but requests like these could only be fulfilled at large banks in the major cities. Here in his humble town (he gestured dismissively) it was impossible. Nevertheless, he was charmed to have made my acquaintance and hoped I wouldn't hesitate to call on him if he could provide further assistance.

⌒

The Shri Meenakshi-Sundareshwarer temple complex in south India encompasses more than half a square kilometre in the centre of the city of Madurai. It is surrounded by six-metre high walls. Each wall contains a *gopuram* (portal) over fifty metres high, visible from throughout the city and the surrounding countryside. Each *gopuram* is covered with thousands of painted figures depicting gods and goddesses, mythological figures, even entire myth cycles.

Sitting in the shade of a banyan tree in a courtyard outside one of the many temples within the complex, I was surrounded by a group of young boys, ranging from perhaps five to twelve years old.

"Hello Madam. What is your name?"

I told them and continued writing in my notebook, hoping to discourage them.

"What is your country?"

"Canada."

"That is near France," one said. "May we have one pen?"

"I only have one pen," I said, gesturing at the notebook and pen in my lap. "How will I write if I give it to you? And Canada is not near France."

"What are you writing?" asked the eldest boy.

"I'm writing about this place, the temples and the shrines and – ahem – the small boys. Maybe it will become a letter, or maybe it will just be something that helps me remember."

"Your country is America?" another boy asks.

"No, Canada is a different country. It is north of America."

"Ah. Near England."

"No. I'll show you." I turned to a fresh page in my notebook and sketched a map of the world, labelling and drawing borders for India, England, France, America and Canada.

"Ah, Canada. Very good place. Very far away."

"Yes. Very far away."

One of the boys interrupted: "I know where China is!" He pointed to an area of the map.

"Then show it on the map," I said and handed him the pen. His face showed his struggle with the temptation to run away with the coveted object.

The eldest boy, seeing the other boy's struggle, preemptively punched him on the shoulder and snatched the pen from him, then pulled the map towards himself. "How does it go?" he asked me.

"C-H-I-N-A," I said, and he wrote it on the map and drew borders.

Another boy said: "I know where Russia is!" The eldest boy, evidently trusting this boy more than the other, gave him the pen with a warning look. Another boy called out "Pakistan," another "Nepal." Each was given his turn at the map. Gradually the map filled up with all the countries we could remember, the pen passing from hand to hand amongst us. We got confused in Africa, so we cheated and divided the continent into three or four big countries. Germany ended up about the same size as Belgium, and Liechtenstein and Luxembourg made the boys roll on the ground with hilarity, both from the absurdity of their size and the challenge of pronouncing their names. They were skeptical of my insistence that Australia sat way down at the bottom-right corner of the world. They were sure it was much closer to England.

The youngest boy's one go at the map – Sri Lanka – was messy, with squiggly lines and illegible letters. His enthusiasm for writing with the pen carried him away into a free-association scribble at the bottom of the page, underway before the other boys could stop him. Scandalized, they expelled him from our cartography game by relegating him to the outside of the circle.

Our map filled up, and I became tired from the heat, the flies, the ceaseless noise and activity around the temple and the exuberance of the boys. I tore the page with the map from my notebook and gave it to the eldest boy.

"Perhaps I will come to Canada one day, Auntie," he said.

"Perhaps you will. Perhaps you will meet some small boys and draw a map with them," I said.

The smallest boy, seeing that we were about to part, could not resist one last attempt. "One pen, Auntie!"

"No pen!" The eldest boy cuffed him across the head. "Friend!"

Subject: Sai Baba Land
From: Janis Harper

To Puttaparthi, Andhra Pradesh, next – off the backpacker track
and thus difficult to get to by land – where the little school is that
I helped start up last year and where Sai Baba lives. Believed to be
India's current *living *avatar* or god-incarnate, his ashram draws
millions of devotees from around the world who fly into the airport
there, made for their convenience. Last year, after I'd returned home
from my first Indian journey, I received an excited phone call from the
head of the school, Ramana, who told me that in a rare interview he was
selected to have with Sai Baba – during which Ramana showed him
pictures of me with the children – the *bhagwan* told him to name the
school after me, if I was willing. The school took my name on Christmas
Day, 2008. Sai Baba is known for his *seva* (service, charity, good works)
and for encouraging it in others, like any good *swami*. Apparently, it
worked on me, without my even realizing it.

Adam and I were unexpectedly met at the train by Ramana, and
immediately wreathed in huge garlands of roses around our necks
like holy people. The Janis Harper Sai REDS English Medium
School is looking good: thirty-six students, aged five to ten, all bright-
eyed and beautiful and happy to see us. "REDS" is an acronym for
"Rural Educational Development Schools" and "English Medium"
does not refer to the paranormal, but to the pedagogy: all lessons are
taught in the medium of the English language, which will ensure
more opportunities for the students later in life. It looks like an actual
school now, with alphabet posters and educational paraphernalia about,
and a full kitchen with all of the implements. There's a lovely photo

of me on the wall – enlarged and framed, with "JANIS HARPER, SCHOOL DONAR" (*sic*) printed in white block letters on the bottom. I guessed it was one of the pictures they took on their cell phone when I was there last year.

We spent much time at the school over the week, eating spicy curries for breakfast made by Ramana's wife, helping serve rice and *daal* to the children and playing English language sing-song games with them, like "Head, Shoulders, Knees, and Toes." The "school photographer" made a DVD of our visit, to help with fundraising in Vancouver, and Ramana had each child stand by me, face the camera and say his or her name and the name of the school: "I go to Ja-NEES Har-PAIR." I then gave each student a pen, pencil and notebook decorated with Canadian maple leaves.

Although many of these children are orphans (because of disease, drought, poverty), they all seem to burst with an unbridled playfulness that I see in Indian children everywhere – that is, when they don't have their heart-wrenchingly mournful begging faces on. This school will get them started in a life where they may not have to play that role to survive. The children are well behaved and orderly in their blue uniforms, disciplined at work under Ramana's strict yet affectionate gaze, and when they gathered for a group photo with me, each one had to touch me, nearly knocking me over with their enthusiasm. I fell in love with each of them.

Ramana kept us busy seeing the sights (all Sai Baba-related, of course) and performing ground-breaking ceremonies for a larger school/care centre where about one hundred orphans could live. I performed *puja* (religious ritual offerings): I broke a coconut in, apparently, the most auspicious way – two even halves – drank its water, smoothed it on my head, offered it to others, and waved incense about, to bless and help spiritually prepare (or smudge, as our "Indians" might say) the five acres of land that were donated for the new school. Ramana wants my friends and family to come in two years, when he believes the school will be built and running. His visions seem to turn to reality (by the grace of the *bhagwan*?): he solemnly showed me the five hundred rupee bill I gave him when I first met him last year; he never spent it, but waited patiently for the fuller fruit of his vision, the larger funding that would come, eventually, from Vancouver, Canada. He always knew it would.

Now he says, the delight in his own imagination widening his already round eyes, "Mom, in two years, Mom, you, your friends, your family come, Mom! You go to *darshan* at temple every day, you come home to your school's guesthouse – made just for you, Mom!" Knowing Ramana, this will likely happen somehow, in some currently unforeseeable way. I don't have any plans to return at that time. But I won't be surprised if I find myself here.

Puttaparthi is a strange, intense little village full of very aggressive beggars (who come from a neighbouring, less affluent village, to prey on the foreign devotees) and late-middle-aged white European women dressed in traditional Indian clothing who live here to be near their Baba. They've created the odd European oasis in restaurants where one can get a good coffee and French pastry and dine in air-conditioned luxury.

An elegant silver-haired German woman who's been living here for ten years told me, "The energy is very, very strong here. They say if you live here you either go stark raving mad or happy. I've chosen the happy side." And another, French, devotee, four years here: "Living here, it's hard on the outside. But I have Sai Baba inside [she pats her chest], so I'm happy."

Like some of the places in India where famous gurus live, the atmosphere in Sai Baba Land is almost cult-like. Although there is no set dogma and proselytizing is not encouraged (you get to keep the religion you came with), most of the devotees I spoke with sounded fanatical and ended up contradicting themselves, as fanatics do. And each had at least one story of being saved, answered or healed – and shared it as soon as we met, as if they were reciting their qualifications. A Canadian woman who lives in Puttaparthi now, after having been healed from a full-body paralysis by Sai Baba (a cross-continental healing: she was in Canada and he was in India), gave me this instruction: "Surrender to him; let him show you the way. He has *way* more love than you or me." Only with complete devotion and surrender to him do you get the gifts, the miracles, in your life. In other words, there's one truth. And you've got to buy the whole cow.

Bema, a serene-faced, young Nepalese woman – a student at one of Sai Baba's free colleges and obviously an intellectual – asked me in impeccable, British-clipped English, "Do you believe in his divinity?"

After some careful consideration I responded, "I believe in his divinity as much as I believe in yours and mine."

She laughed. "That's just what Sai Baba would say." But she pressed further: "What about all of his documented miracles?"

I answered truthfully, "My life is full of miracles."

She then went on to describe how he is of a "higher vibration" than any other being, spiritual practice or religion.

Certainly the Indians in and around Puttaparthi believe in Sai Baba's divinity – that he is the reincarnation of the holy Sai Baba of Shirdi and responsible for countless miracles – and the locals have grown up accustomed to having God actually living on their doorstep. And of course, Sai Baba is great for business: Puttaparthi rakes in the spiritual-tourist dollars. Even so, shopkeepers stop conducting business and run eagerly into the street if his car happens to roll past; they close their businesses to attend *darshan*; and they take genuine pride in recounting his miracles and philanthropic works. Sai Baba has devotees all over the subcontinent, as well as the world.

If you're not a devotee yourself, it feels as if everyone knows you're an imposter, so you do all you can to blend in. Adam and I would attend daily *darshan*, where we'd sit with thousands of others, mostly Indians: males dressed in all-white cotton tunics and trousers in one section, and females in their best, most colourful silk *saris* in a separate section of Sai Baba's opulent, pastel pink-blue-gold temple confection, where pigeons fly about the impossibly high ceiling. The temple looks like it came straight out of a Disney animation.

We'd sing and chant and wait for him to be driven onto the raised stage in his luxury silver car and wheeled out in his chair, and just be in his presence for a while. *Darshan* means "glimpse of God," and here he is: in his early eighties, a bright saffron-orange robe draped over his now-bulging body and a big, fluffy Jimi Hendrix afro haloing his round face. The energy changes, intensifies, and ripples run through the seated crowds. Some murmuring women rise and are forced back down. I can sense the prayers flying to him over my head. And then we settle into more singing and chanting, only this time it's different.

After *darshan*, Adam and I would meet up and eat coconuts from a stall in the huge, sprawling ashram where the temple is located. Like a village itself, the ashram has dorms for thousands of visiting devotees, several restaurants (males and females eat separately), a museum about the world's religions with at least one floor dedicated to Sai Baba, and the guru's own pastel pink-blue-gold Disney-esque mansion.

There are many restrictions in this place, for security and propriety. At one *darshan*, the stern, young, female overseers sent me to a third section in the temple, way at the back with the outcasts, because the sleeves on my dress were not quite long enough. I watched two elderly, wizened and obviously very poor Indian friends get separated: one was sent to the outcast section because she wasn't wearing a blouse (*choli*) under her *sari*, and the other was ushered to the main section, where the protocol is upheld. The woman who was dressed acceptably promptly marched back to the outcast section, plopped herself down on the marble floor beside her friend and matter-of-factly removed her own blouse! The overseers were confounded. Her long breasts dangled defiantly, peeking out from beneath the colourful cotton folds of her *sari*, and she shot a joyful, crooked-toothed grin in my direction. I felt like cheering.

Adam and I were grateful to escape the spiritual intensity into HBO's American movies on our hotel TV in the evenings.

*Sai Baba died in 2011, two years after this visit, and the foreign devotees disappeared from Puttaparthi. The town has sunk into poverty. The school is now in a neighbouring rural village, and there are one hundred and seventy students and four teachers.

Subject: Marriage?

From: Ashlee Petrucci

As part of my volunteer work in Tamil Nadu, I have the great privilege of visiting small towns in order to meet the women who are part of the micro-credit program. The women hold weekly meetings to discuss the status of their loans and share with the group their successes and concerns. Every meeting is the same. I walk through the town, my blonde hair and petite stature a blazing reminder of everything I am and everything that I am not. The children either run forward in excitement to practice their English, or they hang back and watch shyly as their braver friends talk to the blonde girl. Whereas the children might be shy, the town's women are not. The other day, my Audrey Hepburn sunglasses were a roaring success during a group meeting. A *sari*-clad woman snatched them from my head and quickly donned them – the biggest grin on her face as we "oohed" and "aahed" over her fabulous accessory.

While my accessories may be a great hit in India, my personal life is often questionable. During one meeting, as I stood amongst *saris*, gold bangles, sweets, juices and incense, a rather robust woman settled herself in front of me and began the inquisition.

"Work?"

"English teacher."

"Ah, teacher. Good, good."

"Marriage?"

"No."

"What? Why, why? You pretty girl. How old?"

"Twenty-six."

"Ah, when I was your age I married five years and two children. Why no marriage?"

"Well, uh, in Canada, many women marry at an older age these days. It's okay."

I had clearly disappointed my questioner. While my job status filled one shoe, my marriage status clearly did not fill the other. This is something I have grown accustomed to in India. My single status is one that causes questionable looks from Indian women and lustful looks from Indian men. As if, when I walk down the street alone, the absence of a man by my side is an invitation to not only stare, but to approach me and begin a mundane conversation about my country, my age and, oh yes, my marital status.

I have quickly learned that answering "Married" is by far the wiser response. However, the lack of a wedding band causes my hopeful suitors to furrow their brows in puzzlement. Nevertheless, my tiny lie sends them away, and I am free to enjoy the sweet smell of chrysanthemum flowers in my hair, the taste of Indian delicacies that make my stomach smile and the spiritual essence that radiates from so many of the beautiful women I encounter.

Subject: Up the Kerala Coast

From: Mariken Van Nimwegen

In India, it's best to expect things hardly ever work out the way you hoped or planned. Sometimes, it's simply like this: like the locals, you sit yourself down in the dust by the side of the broken bus, you shut your mouth, close your brain and aim your eyes at the horizon, then you just wait. It's one of life's important ego-busting tests. It also manages to stretch your senses, check your opinions and self-knowledge, reach out to the "other" world around you, a world where faith and karma still rule. "Reason" is not what leads you to creativity, nor does it reopen long-blocked channels to your heart.

India is an exhilarating, endlessly interesting but exhausting place. I can't wait to embrace its edge and its grit again, to gain new direct experience. To feel so alive.

In my element,

Mariken

⌒

My dear friends,

Wishing you could all join me for a little while on the public buses through rural Tamil Nadu and Kerala, to get the flavour of the "method" in the traffic madness. If there's indeed a hidden pattern, it must simply be first-come-first-go or who has the sharpest bumpers or loudest horn. Nobody ever slows down; yielding to anybody is out of the question. Keeping to your side of the road is open to interpretation. Driving is a matter of going full speed ahead and anticipating the path of moving pedestrians, cows, chickens, auto-rickshaws, lorries, buses and cars.

Two overloaded old-model buses approach each other head-on, full speed on the available one-and-a-half lane of rural roadway until, at the last possible instant, they fishtail past each other. Shocking. You quickly understand that any sudden or irregular moves, by anyone, are deadly. Chickens and dogs that are still alive seem to know that as long as they keep going steady, things go fine. Better for you to look out the bus's side window to try to enjoy the beauty of the landscape.

Don't worry about the pedestrians in Indian cities, dodging all over the roads in the midst of traffic. Nobody stops for them as they do in Canada, and they're very good at tucking in briefcases, bellies and toes when they zigzag between waves of belching, honking cars, buses and bikes. If you're old or timid, or disabled, you won't get across, that's all.

Quite aside from this dance of death in traffic, there's a "social dance" taking place inside the bus, where the sexes are strictly segregated and seats re-arranged when new people enter the bus: men sitting next to men in the back of the bus, women with women in the front, or, if absolutely no other scenario can be arranged, you may sit next to a young boy or an old man (presumably a safe, non-sexual situation). In this tight, overcrowded situation, he will be sitting uncomfortably on one cheek, his back half turned to you, sometimes for hours, painfully suffering his culture's social taboos.

On the other hand, the residual colonial behaviour I still experienced in 1981, where people usually gave the foreigner the best seat and deferred in so many ways, is gone, and just as well. On the contrary, in modern India, young people can be brash and impolite, coming straight up to you, hand outstretched, asking where you are from, what your name is, shouting "Hi!" with an obvious American-film accent, joking and giggling.

Then again, sometimes it's like you don't exist at all – to some people you're simply invisible. This is much more unsettling. For a waiter in a restaurant to simply ignore you until you finally make an exasperated noise tests severely your capacity for mood change. Also, why is it that numerous other foreign travellers you pass on the street are incapable of even saying hello in answer to your beaming smile? What causes them to look so morose, so hard-bitten? Did they overdose on India's exasperations to a point beyond joy, let alone normal polite conduct? Why are they here, then? It remains one of life's mysteries.

Tourists, predictably and too often, are pre-occupied with their cameras, looking grim and uptight on a self-imposed but urgent mission. I attended a Kathakali dance performance in Kerala recently, and I nearly exploded because of the incessant flash photography in the faces of the actors trying to perform this very precisely detailed art form, my view spoiled by numerous arms outstretched above heads, as is the digital camera practice.

To travel the way I do, short-hopping from town to town on public transit, is to be dependent on numerous kind little gestures and helpful hints from the locals – you simply can't know which bus to take when its sign is written in Tamil or Malayalam script. You need to ask, and kind gestures come in spades. A perma-smile on my face helps.

Days are filled with a continuum of events from the bizarre to the sublime, a cliché that was likely coined in India. All manner of details are there for the bus rider to enjoy.

The new-house architecture that has developed its own indigenous style in the last few decades is a trip to watch. I can only describe it as Third World Miami-Moderne meets Nouveau-riche Château-esque with Muslim or Hindu flourishes added to the Grecian classics. You build your villa in one of two materials: concrete or plastered-over brick. Air conditioning is a must. So is a big fence around it all.

Then there's the marvel of the tropical plants, the same kind we beg and cajole to grow in little pots inside our houses in Canada: combine them in the yard, ignore them over the years and the ensuing jungle soon reclaims a collapsed old house, of which there are many. Nobody is interested in old houses anymore, which is too bad because the traditional Kerala houses are well proportioned, beautifully textured, built with organic materials, open, airy and thus cool by design. India's heritage is disappearing fast. Cityscapes are mired in contrasts, from the ancient temple towers called *gopurams* to hyper-modern office towers, observed in one sweeping glance.

People-watching in India is truly superb. Look at the eccentric ways in which, for instance, men constantly re-arrange their draped, untailored *lunghis* while upholding proper British dress standards of black umbrella, dress shoes and socks, ever-crisp shirt covered by a woollen vest underneath a tweed jacket. If you're lucky, you'll see a more extreme case of the mendicant *sadhu* who not only goes around near-naked, hair knee-length in dreadlocks, but quite literally sticks his head in the sand for religious alms.

This is a population so full of contradictions, it's as though it's still adjusting to rapidly heightened living standards and global exchange; so utterly bourgeois sometimes, so parochial in its own culture, and yet, particularly in the case of adolescent males, so keen to be hip, both in western dress and pop language.

Upon my return I'll show you some portraits of the electrical and telephone wiring of old that makes you wonder what's more genial: these enormous tangles of wires or the smart act of going wireless. If Indians could only find a way to do pipeless plumbing in the future, too, many of India's problems would be solved, and I don't mean returning to the system of poor untouchables going around the town's households to collect slop. Like in China, the sheer population pressure is alarming and in your face. Urban systems have nowhere nearly kept pace. The garbage problem threatens to overwhelm the country these days, almost to the point of catatonic block. The simple medieval system of roaming goats, cows and dogs eating the organic garbage expelled from the houses in the city's streets still works, but the newfangled plastic-bag-and-bottle problem is plain scary.

I've been here now close to one month. I soak it all up like a sponge. In my first week, I met the Dalai Lama giving a loose and giggly speech at the Auroville community on the Tamil Nadu coast; just a few days ago I was hugged – twice! – by Amma, the widely revered "Hugging Mother," at the Amrita Ashram near Kollam on the Kerala coast. I'm not sure these qualify as big events, as some people would have it, but if it's meant to help me feel good, it worked.

I'm inching my way up the Kerala coast by local bus, travelling a distance of sixty to a hundred kilometres every second or third day. Perhaps I'll run into another reasonably fast computer sometime soon and offer you the next long list of vignettes.

Mariken

Subject: Haunts of Ancient Peace
From: Janis Harper

Adam's first Indian train ride, heading south to Hampi, Karnataka: Late at night, we find our reserved sleeper berths in the eight-berth coach and are the first ones there. Cockroaches roam the wall, right where we'll lay our heads when we sleep. An old toothless beggar with unusable twisted legs swings himself by his hands on the floor – horror-movie-style – and begs for money at our feet. Then the *hijras* come clapping: flamboyant, *sari*-clad transsexuals who have made themselves into "women" – and some, not only in dress. They tease Adam and aggressively demand money, ostensibly to lift curses or confer blessings, we find out later. Apparently they do weddings. (They are considered a "third sex" in India and have their special place in society, like everyone seems to.) But the cockroaches, the beggars and now the *hijras* are a bit much all at once for Adam's first train experience. We decide to try to move to the more elite and quiet air-conditioned section, to escape the surreal crowds in Second-Class Sleeper, but officials send us back to our reserved carriage. Reluctantly, we return – only to find that it's now full of foreigners like us! India: difficult, strange, sometimes frightening, and then suddenly familiar and comfortable.

Then came the monsoon that devastated Karnataka, and we barely made it to Hampi. We were forced to get off of our train and board a small, local train from a little village. As I squeezed, guitar on my back, into the train with hundreds of pushing, shoving, mostly male Indians (some of whom apparently hadn't see a western woman up close before), I felt men's hands under my clothes, up my long skirt and

thighs, under my shirt to my breasts. The man or men were groping
me from behind, circling to the front of my body, and by the time
I understood what was happening – Those are hands on my flesh?
Whaaa? – and cried out, it was over, and the crowd had dispersed
on the train.

A strange thing: when I became aware of the hands on my skin, for
an instant I thought they were a lover's hands; they seemed gentle
and familiar. The next instant I felt fear and then anger – what a
violated woman is supposed to feel. I was shaken by the experience.

After the train and one rickety rickshaw that waded slowly through
the flooded streets, we arrived in the quiet, sacred city of Hindu ruins,
Hampi. Hampi was a haven – and although the river was raging red
from the earth and had overflown into a few riverside restaurants,
not much damage was done. It had rained hard for forty-eight hours
straight, for the first time there in nineteen years, we were told.

A sacred site for centuries, the calm in Hampi is palpable, and a kind
of magical peace pervades everything – or, as our local friend Krishna
put it, "Hampi is like heaven." I've never seen the kind of light that's
in Hampi: it turns everything a soft gold. And I'm reminded of Van
Morrison's song, "Haunts of Ancient Peace."

I was happy to renew old acquaintances with the handsome, friendly
waiters and shop owners who remembered me warmly from last year,
and wander about amid the Hindu temple ruins and ancient
monuments that are everywhere you turn. The Indians who live there
hang their colourful laundry from the crumbling temple pillars.

Hampi's landscape is other-worldly: reddish-brown boulders of
all sizes, many gigantic, piled on top of each other, some in
precarious tower arrangements. No one knows how they came to be
there, though there's an explanation that involves the monkey
warrior-king/god Hanuman throwing the boulders from his hilltop
temple in the war that's documented in the *Ramayana* epic. We
climbed the six hundred and twenty steep concrete steps to
Hanuman's tiny whitewashed temple, guided by Mowgli, a young
man who really could talk to the many monkeys we met on the way

up, and kindly eased our relations with these assertive little creatures. The view from Hanuman's perch was astounding: boulders balancing every which way, forming strange contours, as far as the eye could see.

In Hampi, Adam got inspired to volunteer at Harmony House, a place where poor children can go to play and eat instead of beg from foreigners on the streets. He also got his ear pierced by hand (a slightly painful experience) and took *djembe* drum lessons. I had a turquoise *salwar kameez* tailor-made for me by the same lovely, round, middle-aged woman who gave me an *ayurvedic* oil massage. She got to know the contours of my body well. Adam and I were "blessed" by the temple elephant, Lakshmi: after giving her a rupee in her trunk that she then gave her handler, she touched our bent heads with her trunk. And I was head-butted in the butt by a cow on the street and actually lifted off the ground by her horns (a slightly unnerving experience). Apparently I was in her way.

One night in the temple courtyard, Adam sat very still as a cow walked right up to him. I stood back, trying to quell my protective motherly instincts and just let the event unfold. She looked meaningfully into his eyes, wagged her head, Indian-style, to show she was friendly, and then bent her head down and gently licked his bare legs and arms with her long cow tongue as he laughed joyfully in the dark, patting her head.

Subject: Green and Yellow

From: Jill Stock

I travelled to India for the first time in January 2000 and to the
Sivananda Yoga Vedanta Dhanwantari Ashram in Neyyar Dam,
Kerala, as Jill, a student of yoga and Yoga Teacher Trainee, an artist
and feminist. I wanted to have a more authentic experience of learning
yoga from its source, in India. I returned to Canada as Janaki, fully
permeated with the "deep green" of India (as my friend said), and the
weight of spiritual responsibility that my new name bore. Janaki is
"Sita" of the epic *Ramayana*. Above all else she is a "real woman,"
suffering as so many women have.

After many subsequent trips to India, I returned to the same ashram
in 2010, exactly ten years later, this time as an experienced teacher.
I found myself, blonde-haired and blue-eyed, on stage before large
groups of foreign students who wished for the same authentic
experience and learning as I had. Because I am a western woman,
the students felt comfortable asking me questions like, "Why did the
Indian masters often write negatively about women the way they did
in the traditional yoga texts?" Indeed, a good question.

From Swami Sivananda, "Sadhana," Divine Life Society, Rishikesh,
Uttarakhand, 1958, pp. 535-536.

> *A Karma Yogi is expected to be very sociable, readily pleasing, cheerful,*
> *adaptable and of pleasant speech. He must know to mix with all,*
> *anticipate one's wants and serve on, day and night. This is all right. But*
> *could this same free attitude be assumed, when moving with members of*
> *the opposite sex? This answer is self-evident. Beware of women.*

Green: Sivananda Ashram, Neyyar Dam, Kerala, January 2000

Today was our first day off, and we took a day trip to the jungle and hiked to a waterfall. It was an absolutely amazing day and very restorative for me; it gave me a sense of normalcy about my life, that there is more than just the ashram. We saw a scorpion, huge centipedes that burn your skin with cold if you touch them, elephant dung (but no elephants) and heard some monkeys (but didn't see them). My favourite *swami* from London was an absolute treasure to be with today. He was swimming and splashing us with water, taking our pictures, trying on my orange sunglasses. He talks very openly about his life. It seems he knew as soon as he received his mantra that he wanted to be a *swami*. This certainty astounds me. We talked about the *Sri Lalita Sahasranama* which was chanted in the Chandiga Homa the other day. Imagine a book, a text that is just a list of goddesses' names, incarnations of the Divine Mother. It makes me think of my work. I imagined myself recording women reciting their common western women's names, like "Vera," "Joan" and "Barbara." I am very happy right now. I do feel a peace and interest in the world that I have not felt in a very long time.

I have been given a spiritual name, Janaki. It's strange because I have taken to the name in a way that I didn't think I would. Swami Saradananda was like a schoolgirl when she gave me my name. She held my shoulders, pulled me towards her and whispered in my ear, "Your name is Janaki. Your name is Janaki. Your name is Janaki." And it did feel like my name was Janaki, and I realized that I was never told that my name was Jill; it was just assumed. I respond to Janaki now, oddly. Everyone who knows me as Jill will soon be leaving the ashram, and I will just be Janaki.

Before I came to India, I prepared myself for the cultural difference: women would be treated differently, and as a foreigner I could anticipate a different treatment still. But I was not somehow prepared for the subtlety with which this happens – expressions of power, intimidation, expressed as a joke. Such contradictions in masculinity: men wear skirts but are very macho and easily wounded. How many contradictions exist here! Billboards for movies and condoms and brassieres with scantily clad women, yet the way women's bodies are protected and covered and the amount of anxiety around the body is huge. Perhaps I am starting to bridge the gap between my life here and my life at home. I am looking at India and seeing it for its negative aspects. I am tired of being so careful all the time. Don't touch anyone, check what you're wearing, what you're saying, what you're thinking . . . for God's sake.

And then there's Savitri. I've learned that apparently her husband tried to kill her by burning her, but she managed to get away. Since then she's lived at the ashram, and she doesn't see her children because they are with her husband. I am overwhelmed at times by other people's lives, but what about my own? My life here is all about discipline. I don't know if this is good or not. How will this be possible when I go home? All I know is that I am quite content here. I am happy. I have no real worries. I am well supported. I'm healthier than I have been in my life. It's probably been two months since I've looked at my watch to see what time it is at home. I'm completely here.

Leaving the ashram, this is what I've learned:
1. Do what you think is right always.
2. Don't worry about what other people think, even in India.
3. Always tell the truth.
4. Learn to forgive, because if you are doing the right thing, you must be able to forgive others.
5. Don't worry about knowing your own heart, it's there already. The answers are all there.

From Swami Sivananda, "Sadhana", Divine Life Society, Rishikesh, Uttarakhand, 1958, pp. 535-536.

You must know that the woman is the Achintya Maya Sakti, meant specially to ensnare and to delude. Gold or money deludes man after he comes in their contact. But woman powerfully draws and pulls down even one who vigilantly remains aloof. No doubt, they are Devis and Mothers. That is for the one who has acquired that vision, not for you. From a distance you can warm yourself in the heat of the fire. But go near, you are destroyed. It will reduce you to ashes. Remember and beware.

This strange fascination exercised by woman is something altogether inexpressible and dangerous. However wise or strong-minded a person may be in other matters, here he succumbs and falls miserably. Do not have any idea of service in connection with woman. This way, you cannot attain salvation. The chances are rather of perdition. Be a Karma Yogi, but remain always as a Sadhaka or as a Brahmacharin that you are and emulate the Sannyasin you are to be.

Yellow: Sivananda Ashram, Neyyar Dam, Kerala, January 2010

On Christmas day, while you were opening presents, perhaps, or sitting by a fireplace, I was having twenty-two "head baths."

A small group of us headed to Rameswaram which is a little filament of Tamil Nadu that stretches towards Sri Lanka. This is where Rama worshipped Lord Shiva and where he is said to have constructed the bridge to Lanka to rescue his wife, Sita. Naturally, since I am looking for Sita myself, this pilgrimage was an important one for me. Satellite photos show something underwater which NASA says is most certainly man-made (and possibly the bridge), so it gives credence to my favourite story.

The temple at Rameswaram has twenty-two different wells which pilgrims take a bath in. How it works is that you hire a guy with a bucket to walk around with you. He drops the bucket down into each well, dumps it over your head and then you move onto the next. The water from each well is said to remove various karmas, including murder. So I'm good to go for the next few lifetimes, I should think!

Then we drove to Dhanushkodi Beach which was destroyed by a cyclone in 1964 but is where the bridge was supposed to have been. A beautiful place. Later, back at the ashram, I got a terrible migraine that lasted three days. Once I'd determined that it was time to chop off my head instead of suffer any longer, Swami Govinda arranged for me to see a homeopathic doctor in the city. The doctor asked me if I'd taken any "head baths" lately. I said, "Yes, twenty-two of them."

India is a great place to develop strength and confidence because people here can seem harsh, they can ask probing questions, they can seem like they're judging, and you have to summon your inner strength and pride in who you are. So what I'm working on at the moment is clarity of purpose, trust and allowing that inner voice out in all situations. Also, I tell myself that it is okay for me to make choices simply because they make me happy; they don't have to be well reasoned. I'd like to throw reason out the window for a bit.

And, yes, I am learning to speak "Indian." Here's an example. "Tomorrow going SP office, today coming evening, talking something" means that tomorrow I will go to the SP office; however, today I am returning and would like to talk to you about something in the evening.

There is, however, a lot that I can't give voice or words to. Let's just say that this trip has broken me of any illusions I might have had about India. I've reached a point where I often forget that I'm not Indian. Not that I blend in exactly, but I feel so comfortable that I feel at home. If someone does stare at me it is somewhat shocking, and I have to remind myself that I'm a foreigner here. A pair of jeans and a Superman T-shirt are doing wonders to bridge the gap between the person I am here and the one I am in Canada. I found I was starting to look more Indian than most Indians, so now I am just myself.

A defining moment: I was leading the *satsang* tonight at the ashram. There are about seventy or so guests at the moment, predominantly western women. I picked up a book by Swami Sivananda and asked the guests to choose the page number that I would read from. A woman called out, "535." I scanned it first to see what it was and noticed that it contained quite a lot about women. Normally I won't read this kind of passage out because it creates too much controversy, but I think it's better to face things than sweep them under the rug. I told the guests that there were some things in that selection that I thought best not to read out. They asked me to "please" read it anyway, and how could I not? My number had come up, so to speak. It was time. I could feel it.

So, why did many of the original teachers of yoga write about women in such a negative way?

I explained that the books were written several decades ago, or more. The role of women, even in western society, was vastly different then, and keep in mind that India would be at least another couple of decades behind in its ideas about possibilities for women outside the home. At that time in India, women rarely followed a traditional path of yoga. They did not leave their families or pursue a formal spiritual path. They found their own way to practice, within the family. The books were written primarily for young men, who might be following a formal path and needed guidance to maintain their vows of *brahmacharya* (or abstinence, control of the senses).

I told the students that, in truth, even understanding this, it was difficult for me to hear and to accept these writings about women. I thought that perhaps we needed, now, to hear more women writing about their experiences on the spiritual path. Swami Sivananda, in his lifetime, did initiate women into *Sannyas* (the *swami* order; like a monk) and did not discourage any woman from pursuing this path. One of the senior male staff who was listening stood up and publicly criticized me for speaking "improperly" about Swami Sivananda, who is considered to be a great saint.

I was shaking. I am still getting used to my role on stage. Although many of the guests come to India expecting to see a great *swami* on stage, perhaps my role as a western woman here is an important one. Yoga teaches me that I am doing my duty, what has been asked of me.

Women, by nature, are different yogis. We filter. I think we are a little more transparent. I have always felt it important to take responsibility somehow for what I teach – not to follow blindly, but to make an effort to integrate and to understand. So even though the books were not written for us, we still take what we need and plod on, resilient.

In the *Devi Mahatmya*, a great battle ensues between good and evil. Brahma, Vishnu and Shiva are called in; however, they are not able to subdue the demons. Finally, they summon Devi who, with her terrific mouth, "extensive tongue" and powers of mantra, is able to swallow every last drop of demon blood to ensure that they could not proliferate.

Perhaps this was my big learning from India: as a woman I have everything I need. I am fearless.

Subject: Further Up the Kerala Coast
From: Mariken Van Nimwegen

Dearests,

It's been more than a month since I wrote to you. Having visited areas where India is still truly timeless, such as the smaller temple towns of south Tamil Nadu and inland Kerala, I often don't pay attention to the date unless I find an English language newspaper. The available computers at internet cafés, often placed in a claustrophobic second-floor spot that resembles a confession booth placed in a sauna, aren't always the greatest, so I apologize for the delay. The fact that the private sector is computerized these days is enough of a miracle, especially when you notice that some government offices continue with the "technology" of the 19th century: two feet tall and wide ledgers filled with flourishing longhand pen-and-ink data.

Kochi, or Cochin, Kerala, is a history-laden place in a beautiful setting on the Arabian Sea coast. Every day I walk for miles, both in Kochi proper, situated on a peninsula, and in its adjacent modern business centre of Ernakulam on the mainland. Kochi is picturesque, mostly, but it's falling apart where it hasn't been restored. Combined with some rude infill built during the last two decades, it's a typical Indian hodgepodge of styles and building heights, but the streets are still reasonably quiet, with some intensely touristy quarters in and around the Old Fort.

Once you travel north of Kochi, tourism virtually disappears, and you're on your own. The Kerala coast becomes increasingly Muslim from there on, populated by an ancient community called the Moplahs. Suddenly the women are covered in austere black robes worn over top of their *salwar kameez* outfits, a very uptight and

171

decidedly un-Indian sight. The main providers of labour in the Gulf States' boom, these people's newly acquired Arab wealth is visible everywhere in the shape of insanely ostentatious mansions going up on the outskirts of towns where the fields used to be. It's fascinating to see how the newly rich Indian's dream mansion tends to share many of the features of the infamous "monster homes" in Vancouver, Canada. Just add Arabic flourishes to the window treatments. Try to imagine these houses painted in Kodak colour-defying chartreuse or full-on magenta, or both, instead of our tepid pink. Then, park a small hatchback car in front, a Maruti (Suzuki Swift), instead of a Mercedes.

I arrive at Thrissur, known as the "culture capital" of Kerala. It's true: every night there are several dance, theatre or musical performances going on, and I'm happily taking in as many folk styles as I can find while I'm here.

Occasionally it occurs to me that I'm probably considered an eccentric, the way I'm running around by myself, even though the locals should know by now that there are many women of my age travelling solo these days. Still, going about alone is hardly an option for Indian women; women almost always walk in groups or are escorted by husbands or other male members of the family.

Tonight, once again, I'm hoofing it home alone. It's around 1:00 AM. Although the town is mostly deserted by now, you're always vaguely aware you're being watched from dark doorways and corridors where some people spend the night. I've almost made it back to the Bini Hotel, a few hundred yards more to go in the dark.

But this time of night, I'm simply too much of a sight. A jeep-full of cops stops alongside me. They ask, assertively, but too obviously curious to be frighteningly official, who I am, where I'm from, where I've been and, by extension, where the heck I'm going alone at this hour. It sounds like they're genuinely concerned about my safety and wellbeing, while I, characteristically, never quite understand what I'm supposed to be so afraid of. I respond with one word only: Kathakali! and point in the direction of the theatre I just came from.

Aha! That explains everything immediately – big grins and bobbing heads all around – enough for me to regain a semblance of legitimacy, if not normalcy. Off the hook suddenly after a few polite exchanges, I quickly disappear into the privacy of my hotel room.

Kathakali performances portray episodes from the *Mahabharatha* sacred texts and always run through the night; the one I attended was by no means finished when I left. It was a "serious" performance presented by the local Kathakali Club for their membership's own delectation, not for tourists, unlike the other photography-inundated show in the Kochi area. This was a roomful of discerning, mainly elderly, *dhoti*-clad gents who were intensely focused on the show, which gave me the chance to intently follow the marvelous interplay between the bizarrely dressed dancers, the drummer, the singer and the dancers' feet whose percussive steps were amplified by ankles full of bells.

Meanwhile, among the regular events in Kerala's daily life, you're likely to encounter a procession of thirty-five caparisoned temple elephants moving around the block, complete with dancing drag queens and elaborate hand-made *papier maché* "Radha and Krishna" love scenes, accompanied by troupes of drummers. That's what I miss on Vancouver's streets sometimes.

Next, I make a brief foray east away from the coast, toward the Western Ghats Mountain Range that separates Kerala from Tamil Nadu, to a town called Palakkad. It's the utterly traditional Brahmin heartland of Kerala and features beautiful, timeless villages such as Kalpathy where I spend a fine afternoon strolling around and chatting with people in doorways here and there. Spontaneously, I undergo an *ayurvedic* massage when I see the opportunity offered at a little local clinic. Delicious, doused all over with hot oil for a deep full-body massage, naked and slippery as a fish on the solid hardwood massage table.

My last, northernmost stop along the Malabar Coast of Kerala is at Bekal Fort, the largest and best preserved coastal fort stemming from the 14th century Vijayanagar Empire. I spend my time taking long, solitary hikes along the beach and through the lush tropical farming compounds along the back roads, knowing I would soon turn inland and away from the ocean for the remainder of my stay in India.

Sunsets on the west coast of India are legendary. When the time comes, you join local families in the relaxed custom of gathering by the waterfront and staring westward into the red globe of the sun, unusually intense, descending as if it were in a race to get to Africa to repeat its glorious performance for the people strolling along the coast of Senegal. In the tropics, sunset is brief, as brief as any extraordinarily beautiful experience should reasonably be, lest we take it for granted and stop searching for it. Within a half hour the pitch dark night is upon us. Ah, those long, balmy tropical nights come to mind, spent in beach restaurants in Goa in 1981, gin-and-tonic in hand, eyeing the impossibly handsome, saronged waiters with their perfect posture, and appreciating, more than ever, The Doors who provide optimal backdrop on the sound system. Loudly. Adding immeasurably to my longing languidity.

⌒

But away from the flashback, to return to Kerala, circa 2009. As it happened, barely three hours of bus travel north of here, in the town of Mangalore in Karnataka, a party of young women students held a celebration at a pub, enjoying a beer together. Hardly an earth-shattering occasion to our western ears, but as it turned out, to some it was still considered a liberal move for young women to make in contemporary India. A local fundamentalist Hindu group of men got wind of it. They swiftly raided the pub and proceeded to verbally and physically attack the women who were rescued by bystanders before anything more serious could happen.

The incident went national and managed to engender a heated discussion in the newspapers about Hindu communal mores and Indian cultural propriety vs. "western-style" individualist modernity. The debate, as usual among the highly volatile and politicized people of India, was fascinating in the way it illustrated the ongoing struggle amongst traditionalists to adapt to a rapidly changing society. The incident fired up the entire range of passionate opinion between liberal secularism, religious sectarianism and cultural conservatism, with a great deal of male chauvinist pomposity thrown in for good measure.

There's a growing reactionary and potentially dangerous political train of thought in India that promulgates a form of nationalism that sees itself as identical with the religion of the majority, Hinduism, and ignores the long-standing historical reality of a relatively harmonious religious pluralism within Indian society. Among many extremist fringe movements in this vein, the more populist mainstream Bharatya Janata Party (BJP) that rules large areas of northern India and regions in the south as well, was founded on the sentiment. How can it be, asks Amartya Sen, the Nobel-prize-winning economist in his book, *The Argumentative Indian*, that citizens so easily forget Gandhi's tenets for a secular, pluralist democracy as the courageous and admirable foundation for an independent India?

Thankfully, in the case of the Mangalore women, many letters to the editor came down on the side of women being their own masters in such an innocuous issue as sharing a social drink, albeit in a theoretically teetotalling, predominantly Hindu environment. Young women all over India came up with the right answer in gender solidarity: they mailed massive amounts of pink panties to the offices of this particularly aggressive Hindutva group.

ↄ

The incident served as especially spicy food for thought at the very time I was in the area. I won't deny the quickly passing but disquieting thought of what could happen should I find myself in the wrong place at the wrong time in this conservative region. As for occasional lewd gestures that the female solo traveller must inevitably endure from certain men, well, I'm laconic about it. It's no different anywhere else in the world. As long as humankind features two sexes with profoundly different abilities, these gestures will continue. It's annoying, but it shouldn't prevent you from striking out on your own. Social discipline still works in India: all you have to do is let the other people around you know, loud and clear, of untoward behaviour. The culprit will be subjected to social discipline, and you'll be rescued.

In northern Kerala, traditional and puritan, people still tend to gape at foreigners the way they used to do anywhere in India in those earlier days. It begins to feel a little claustrophobic for me – the kind of six-foot-tall female they never get to see, a rare specimen and an obvious escapee from the tourist zoo down south.

175

I notice that I'm beginning to get a little cranky at the unwanted attention, a sure sign of emotional and mental fatigue. I have, by now, a head full of impressions and nobody to debrief or discuss them with in depth. I've been unable to find compatible fellow travellers to share a joke with and laugh out loud – most of them are in highly protective group tours and get whisked around briefly and efficiently.

I've spent weeks on end in silent observation, merely conducting simple and short conversations with various hotel and bus company employees. I've consistently dressed properly to suit the host culture, which means you forget about your feminine self by demurely hiding your curves in loose-fitting, body-covering clothing. In so many ways, I try to always fit in and adapt, to be polite and accommodating.

I remember my bouts of deep loneliness here, during my first long solo trip. At that age, I was still testing my mettle on the road in general, as well as discovering my boundaries of self-containment and inner strength under the pressures of being in a completely alien and exotic locale. I'm older now, have done lots of travelling in the third world, and I think I know who I am and what makes me tick. I'm a frequent and voracious socializer, but need episodes of pure silence in between. I now know that I'm fine in my own company, that I love autonomy and anonymity, and that I welcome solitude, even when surrounded by noisy crowds. Just sitting on a bench, being there, looking around and observing the scene for long times feels good. To fill the time during long nights alone in cheap, austere hotels, I've learned to work on my drawings or read and write about the place I'm travelling in.

Solo travel makes for an intense level of concentration on and awareness of the place you're in. This is dissipated to a degree, or just plain different, when you're with a group, friend or partner. I have grown to like being alone, but hardly ever feel lonely anymore.

Mariken

GOA

Subject: Palolem Paradise

From: Janis Harper

Now we are in Palolem, South Goa – a beach resort that attracts
mainly UK and European backpackers and, more recently, the new
middle-class Indian families on holiday. Palolem is quintessential
Goa. And anything goes in Goa. Because of the Portuguese
influence, this small, affluent state is mainly Christian, so all kinds
of meat are available (yes, including the otherwise sacred cow!) and
alcohol is plentiful and cheap, unlike in most other parts of Hindu-
Muslim-Sikh India. No wonder western tourists flock to beautiful,
beach-laden Goa and have been doing so since the hippie era. And
for some, the combination of seemingly limitless freedom and
available substances has nightmarish results, like jail, insanity, death.
India has kept many a wayward traveller for herself.

I'm sitting on the sand, writing this letter in my journal, on the quiet
end of the beach, in the shade of a big rock – the warm Arabian Sea
lapping a few metres away and the main part of the beach to my left,
stretching long and curvaceous, fringed by coco palms and the odd
mammoth banyan tree. Postcard-perfect. We've been here almost a
week, and when we arrived it was a ghost-town beach. Although lots
of tourists were around, only a few restaurant-bars and their adjoining

"coco-hut" guesthouses were on the beach, unlike last year at this time when there were at least a hundred up and running. The restaurateurs just recently got licences to build – only temporary structures are allowed on the beach, so each year it's recreated – and now we're watching the Palolem Beach I knew last year come back to life. Soon, most of these open-air restaurants should be ready, and I can visit my favourite ones (with likely the same waiters!), once they exist again. The temporal nature of things is made very visible in India; permanence is indeed an illusion. And restaurants get reincarnated.

Meanwhile, one weekly event already up at this early time in the tourist season is the "silent disco" or "headphone party." Noise laws prevent plugged-in music after 10:00 PM here, so at the open-air Alpha Bar people rent headphones to hear DJ-ed music and dance around, silently and wildly, to the same tunes blasting in their ears, the British DJs doing their thing on a stage in front of a computer-generated light show. A surreal scene. It goes on all night, and Adam returned at noon the next day, after breakfasting and swimming with some vivacious Irish women he'd met. The party scene is strong here – and young, of course – and Adam is learning how to pace himself and avoid the dangers of "FOMO" or Fear Of Missing Out, as a South African woman explained. He's very friendly and immensely popular and is always introducing me to new friends. I'm known as his "cool mom" (well, one young Irishman called me a "hot mom," but he was drunk).

The headphone parties are more of a youthful domain, and I wait for the live music jams and open mikes to start up, where a large crowd of foreigners will gather at a restaurant-bar and listen to other foreigners, like me, play their music. So, at night I frequent the restaurants that have been built this early in the season, many of which are right on the beach: I sit at a candle-lit table in a comfortable rattan chair with my feet in the sand and the dark sea crashing a few metres away. The menus are similar and extensive, and I order anything I want – traditional Indian food, Goan food, seafood; Thai, Italian, Chinese, and Israeli dishes (all "Indian style," of course); and beer, cocktails, brandy, rum – served by handsome, young and attentive waiters.

This is truly a single woman's paradise. The young men keep me company if it looks like I might like some; they flatter me, are curious about me, want to meet up with me after work. But I'm never quite sure if they're being sincerely friendly or flirtatious or if they just want my business or maybe something else. I've heard that relationships of all kinds occur between young Goan men and western women (of all ages), and I'm wary. Apparently some want a financial "sponsor," so that they can get a work visa and a ticket to a western country; some want the prestige of having had sex with a white woman; and others are hopeless romantics, Bollywood-style, and perhaps the most dangerous.

But how can I know anything for sure? It seems that everyone wants something from me here. Usually it's money. Sometimes it's sex. I don't want to be gullible, an easy mark, the topic of gossiping Indian men who compete with each other over the number of western women they can bed in a season, nor do I want to be rude and push away the very people I came here to be among, due to notions of propriety or out of wariness or fear. It's the female traveller's tightrope walk: safety is important – keeping the eyes straight ahead, no contact – but so is knowing when to look around. Because you just might miss something beautiful. Like a moment of true friendship with a gorgeous Goan waiter.

Sometimes at these beautiful restaurants with the beautiful waiters, I just get tired of trying to figure it all out, and keep my eyes glued to my book to ward off any contact. But there's rarely any real pressure, and it's often just fun. And I do return to those restaurants that my favourite waiters work in. Most of them seem to be named Raj.

My favourite Raj has an impish face, glinting black pearl eyes and long, curly hair – black, of course, and coconut-oily. The wet look. I think he applies the oil a few times a day. He gave me a pretty polished-stone necklace and wants to come to Canada to be with me. He also wants my babies, even though I've explained very clearly to him that, *in any case*, the time for that has definitely past. Once, while illicitly visiting me in my coco-hut, he leaned back against the wall and when he straightened up, there was a large dark spot on the wall.

A wet spot. When I pointed it out to him, he said, "It's my mark." Later I wondered if he meant that he was marking his territory, like a dog.

How could Raj even exist in Canada, in Vancouver? I'd have to line my couch and chairs with towels. And tell him to keep away from the walls.

So Adam and I get to know some of the locals, and I befriend a few of the beautiful women who sell jewellery on the beach to support their five young children and "no-good husbands who don't work." Again, I don't know if this is just a line to get my sympathy and hence business, or if it's true. During our conversations stories of abuse come out, and so does my purse. But if I chance upon the woman with her husband and children later, their evident ease and happy-family feeling tell a different story. But, again, does it really matter what's "true" and what's not? Everyone here needs my money more than I do – that's what's true.

Adam plays soccer on the beach at sunset with Indian guys from the local soccer team; he reads *Shantaram* and does his grade eleven school work online; I practice yoga on the beach (sometimes to the applause of watching Indians: "Very good!"), play guitar and sing, read and write. We both swim in the sultry sea, eat delicious food, have long philosophical discussions and get constantly amazed by the natural beauty and just by being here. We make our way through slow-moving crowds of cows and jumpy gangs of mangy, battle-scarred dogs, avoid the mischievous monkeys and wild rickshaws and motorbikes, and negotiate our way amid the many touts and shop-owners: "Madam, come look my shop! Just looking now, very cheap!" And, every few steps, "Hello, taxi?" "Hello, rickshaw?" "Not today, maybe tomorrow?" Our rooms sometimes become a little zoo; the odd cockroach, spider and hopping frog come to visit.

As I write to you, some monkeys are playing in the trees behind me, and the crows that last year at this time, in autumn 2008, seemed to cry "Ba-RACK, Ba-RACK!" now just "Caw." The light is fading into Goa's smoky haze, the sun is turning neon pink, and I need to find Adam and walk back through the gentle surf to the main beach before the incoming tide turns my sandy pathway to water. I think I'll eat *channa masala* tonight.

Subject: Good Business
From: Denyse Johnson

"You give me price, then I give you price, then we make sale. Is good for you?"

While small in stature and only seventeen years old, Kavita is a bully when it comes to business. Her innocent teenage smile and persistent ways have already convinced me to buy a pashmina scarf, anklet and jewel-covered pen from her kiosk, which she runs with her aunt off the main tourist road of Colva Beach in Goa.

Slightly annoyed at myself because I really don't need any more souvenirs, but mostly amused watching her salesmanship in action, I make up every excuse I can think of why I must leave. She peers at me as though reading my mind and starts talking about her family: her mother who is ill, her father who is an alcoholic and her younger brother whom she often takes care of for weeks at a time while her parents are away. A glint in her almond-shaped, black eyes reveals she knows she has found my weak spot.

"Come with me," she says, grabbing my arm. "I have a special collection for sale at home. I only invite my most favourite customers to see."

I don't move at first, even though she starts walking, and I lose sight of her lime-green, cotton outfit and high-pinned bun as she turns a corner. Realizing I am not behind her, she stops. If I have learnt anything in India, it is that sometimes saying no is just not worth the energy. She waits impatiently as I catch up and leads us past a small church, around a narrow, winding gravel road, along a field of tall grass and a few roaming cows.

As we cross a brick passageway that leads to her home, a middle-aged lady walks past us wearing a multi-coloured, Indian-styled, cotton dress. It looks like a patchwork of mismatched fabric and clashes with the red and white bangles that decorate both her arms. Chunky silver jewellery hangs off her neck, ears and nose, and her dark hair is tied with a thin rope into two sleek pigtails. On anyone else, the outfit would have looked ridiculous, but on her it looks sophisticated and exotic.

"This my aunt," Kavita introduces us. "She looks just like my mom."

A moss-covered, concrete wall surrounds about a dozen small homes that make up Kavita's community. Her house is built of neatly stacked bricks, with uneven pieces of lumber placed side-by-side, making up the roof. Before we step inside, she takes off her shoes and looks at my feet, gesturing for me to do the same. The house costs about one thousand rupees a month to rent, she tells me, and part of what she makes from selling helps to pay for it.

The home is divided into two rooms. The larger room is the one we first enter and is the size of a small North American bathroom. It is filled with bags of rice and stacks of wooden boxes. A thick piece of string with drying clothes draped over it divides the room.

Kavita leads me to the second room, which is only slightly less packed and smells of kerosene. One wall is covered with stacks of bags, while the other displays representations of Hindu gods. The adjacent corner is the kitchen – a few pots and pans, a kerosene cooker and pieces of dehydrated fish, which I politely reject when she offers them. Changing the subject from the food, I ask Kavita about the Hindu gods.

"There's really only one god," she says, with a maturity well beyond her years. "My god, your god, they're all the same – one god with one hundred names."

When I ask where she and her family sleep, she points to the spot where I am standing. The tiny clearing of hard dirt is where all four of them sleep, side by side. The mats they use for beds are rolled up and tucked away among the piles against the walls.

Kavita grabs several bags and dumps them onto the floor. Sitting down cross-legged, she opens them, revealing necklaces, bracelets and other trinkets. Several of the pieces are identical to ones I have seen in the markets I have visited since arriving in India almost a month ago, but she insists that hers are unique – that each and every piece is made by her grandmother. Aqua blues, emerald greens, yellows, brass and silvers brighten up the otherwise unlit room. She lays them out carefully and picks out a chunky bronze chain with a diamond-shaped blue bead.

"You want?" she says in a tone that is more like a statement than it is a question.

I rummage through the pile of jewellery and pick out a long brass chain dotted with emerald green beads. "Good choice," she approves, "but better with earrings." I nod my head in a polite no, which she interprets as the Indian head-wobble meaning yes and pulls out a pair of earrings.

Laughing, I hold up the necklace and make my first offer: one hundred and fifty rupees. She lets out a little squeak. I am her first customer, and first customers are lucky, so I will get the lucky price of five hundred rupees, she insists. We bargain for a few minutes until finally agreeing on three hundred rupees.

"You are good business, Canada," she says, shaking my hand with a firm grip. I put the necklace in my purse, knowing that I have likely paid too much, that I will probably never wear it, and smile. I help Kavita roll the mats of jewellery and place them back against the wall.

As we walk outside she looks at me and tilts her head. "Come," she says leading the way back to the winding road. "Maybe you have time for more shopping. You need *sari*?"

Subject: Bicycles and Bare Breasts

From: Ulrike Rodrigues

The beaches of Candolim are about fifteen kilometres from my uncle's house in Porvorim, but at least forty-five minutes on my India-bought, one-speed Atlas Supreme bicycle.

I like the beachy laneways in Candolim because they're hard-packed and too narrow for anything but the slimmest car. Pedalling along them is a relief because the souvenir and fresh-fruit and ice-cream vendors are usually teens who spend the day catching up with their friends. They're less aggressive than their main street counterparts. They're also usually girls and they grin at my ladies' Indian bicycle with its pink plastic basket and call out, "Nice cycle!" when I pedal past.

I turn the bicycle onto one of the laneways that lead to the beach, and at the end of the lane, grassy, sandy dunes pick up where the road leaves off. I lock my bike to a signpost that points to the Bob Marley Shack and head the opposite way. My feet sink in the soft sand, and I slip off my dusty white Crocs. The surrounding trees form a leafy corridor, and as I continue west towards the Arabian Sea in the late afternoon sun, the beach shacks emerge. I stand and take it all in – the gorgeous, relaxed touristy-ness of one of Goa's famous beach stretches.

To the left and to the right, as far as the eye can see, palm leaf and bamboo pole "shacks" line the beach. Each shack is actually a respectably sized open-air restaurant area with ceiling fans, padded rattan chairs and inexpensive Goan seafood. After the monsoons have passed, shack owners pay the Goan government an exorbitant amount for a licence, build their shack for the November to March season, lay out lounge chairs close to the water's edge and wait.

They wait for the air-conditioned buses of mainly British and Russian "package tourists" to wander into their own little patch of sand, and they serve them hand and foot. By the end of the day, the lounge chairs are strewn with big, flabby, relaxed bodies – brown and white, men's and women's, covered and uncovered.

I perch on the edge of a lounge chair and watch a wandering cow and her calf nuzzle the hands of a fellow in the neighbouring lounge chair. He is brown, and it looks like he's been there a while. His girlfriend is paler, but her nipples are brown. I know this because – contrary to Goan modesty, custom and law on beach attire – she is naked from the waist up. She lies on her back, eyes closed, her white breasts flopping on either side of her chest like a couple of eggs, sunny side up.

She is surrounded by people, but she's chosen to be oblivious to them and go topless here in her own private Eden. No one – including the shack owner – is about to tell her this is inappropriate. To the contrary, when the boyfriend paid for an arm-and-leg massage, the shack owner positioned himself to ensure a close and continuous view. I remembered something I'd read in a book recently: in India, women don't get naked, even when they're being intimate with their husbands.

The shack owner's stare at the woman's chest – intent and unabashed – is familiar to me. It's the look people (mostly men) give me when I ride by on my bicycle. In western countries, women on bicycles are a common sight, and, as the bicycle becomes a popular mode of transportation, more women are doing away with sports clothes and riding in dresses and heels. It's flirty and sexy, they say, and they feel free.

In Goa, you don't see women riding bicycles, especially for transportation. You see women on foot, buses and motorbikes, in *saris* or *salwar kameez* (the combination of loose-fitting pants and flowing tunic). You might see a foreign tourist on a rental bike or a traveller on a tour bike. But you won't see an Indian woman on a bicycle.

Is a bicycle the equivalent of bare breasts? I wonder. Am I bringing my western ideas of transportation to the streets the way western women bring their nudity to the beach? In my shorts, short-sleeved shirt and "work bike" am I trying to prove something? That bicycles are . . . what? Fun? Freeing? Environmental?

Here in Goa, the only people who ride a bicycle are those who can't afford anything else. They carry eggs, milk, propane, cardboard, ladders and people. Workers ride them and old men and children. Sometimes you see a man in office clothes on a bicycle, but his jaw is set. You wonder if he is saving for a motorbike or car.

And I wonder if I am inadvertently mocking them – like first-world backpackers who dress like third-world peasants. A wealthy foreign woman on a plain Indian work bike? What is this – low-caste chic?

I told a Goan writer recently that the big thing in North America is the "hand-built" bike. I showed him a copy of *Momentum Magazine* from Vancouver, Canada, and pointed to a photo of a plain utility bike. A woman in a dress and heels was draped over it. "That bike, there," I said, "that could cost up to ninety thousand rupees." His eyes popped. Minimum wage is one hundred and ten rupees a day.

The longer I'm here, the more I'm mortified with how my culture toys with the bicycle.

My job here in Goa is not to show Indians that bicycles are fun and free and environmental, I tell myself. They've been there, done that, and in so many respects they put North Americans to shame. My job is not to show Indian women that cycling is sexy, either. They look sexy enough carrying their children to school on a 50cc scooter, groceries resting between their knees, *kameez* blowing in the wind.

To be honest, some days I wonder what the hell I'm doing on a bicycle. I draw stares and comments – and I'm not the attention-grabbing sort. In India, isolated from my North American fellow-cyclists, I struggle to hold the faith: "bicycles are great!"

Then it gets down to the most base and selfish reasons: it feels good. Like topless sunbathing, I guess.

En route

Subject: Returning to India
From: Bronwyn McBride

After twenty hours couch-surfing in Kuala Lumpur, I arrived back at the international airport in Delhi. There, I followed a group of turbaned Sikhs and their wives to the flight departure gate.

In the air, I had tried to sleep but was too exhausted and couldn't. So I walked around like I was at a cocktail party, except that everyone else was sitting and no one else was talking or sipping drinks.

The flight landed in Delhi an hour and a half before my next flight – to Mumbai, my temporary home. I could barely get off the escalator that lowered to Immigration, blocked by an enormous line-up of other foreign people also wanting to be in India. In the line, American businessmen discussed their domestic flight schedules for their week of meetings in Pune and Bangalore. In another, much shorter, line-up, fat diplomats fanned themselves with their special passports, complaining about the unsatisfactory air-conditioning.

The mustachioed official almost didn't let me in. He said, as I might have predicted, that I had to stay out of the country for two months before I could return: a brand new rule that was only occasionally enforced. In anguish, I told him about my visit to the foreigner registration office in Varanasi and how the official there had said that my visa was stamped in such a way that I should be allowed back in without any issues.

The clerk shook his head in a way that could have meant yes or no and summoned another official.

"I have another flight at 10:40," I said softly in Hindi, wanting to cry.

The other official arrived and started to grill me. "What are you doing in India? How do you know Hindi?"

I said I'd come to visit friends and see the sights (foolproof, safe answers) and then made a mistake.

"I learned Hindi from a teacher."

He flipped out. You cannot study any subject without a student visa! We argued while other people walked blissfully past me to the baggage claim area.

He looked at my previous Indian visas and suggested that I was secretly conducting business. I said something to the effect of, "Please sir, respected sir, I didn't mean to break any rules. I've never conducted business in India, it was not my intention to do anything wrong, please let me pass, sir, please."

He wanted to see my return ticket out of India. I didn't have one at all, but I said that I didn't have a printout. He told me that I could be sent back (to Malaysia again? What?) on the very same flight. I pleaded with him. I had a connecting flight to Mumbai in less than an hour.

The original official finally let me through, saying my Hindi was very sweet and respectful and that I should register at the Foreigners Office in Mumbai and always choose the correct visa for my purposes. Of course.

By then it was 10:08. I sprinted to the baggage claim area and waited anxiously, squinting through the crowd of people. My baggage claimed, I ran to the shuttle bus depot to go to the domestic airport, a ten-minute ride. I had no printout of my next flight ticket though, and so I was not admitted. The official guard *wallah* slumped on his chair as though it was a bed and gestured towards the prepaid taxi booth, where five other nice people were waiting (in a clump, not a line) at the counter. My god.

When it was my turn, I said I needed to go to the domestic airport, fast. I put money on the dirty counter.

"Your good name?" the khaki-clad clerk asked.

"B-R-O-N-"

He looked up for a moment. " ... Bee?"

"YES. Then ARR, then OWE." I rolled my "R" Indian-style, hoping to speed up the process.

Outside, I fought through a bunch of unprepaid taxi *wallahs* to find the prepaid booth. The taxi driver took his time loading my bags into the car.

"Very heavy!" He smiled and laughed and crinkled his eyes. I was going crazy.

"I'm very late, let's go immediately, quickly." It was almost a lost cause. It was 10:25, and I was in a cab and had still to get there and check in and drop my bags and board a plane that was scheduled to *take off* fifteen minutes later.

"Don't worry," the taxi *wallah* said cheerfully as we hurtled down the road. "Just stay in the airport, you can take a flight in the morning, nice and relaxed." I shrugged, defeated.

When we finally arrived, I loaded my bags onto a cart and ambled over to the check-in counter at a leisurely pace.

"I've missed my flight," I announced to the boy behind the desk, who looked about eighteen. "What do I do now?" But as I spoke, my eyes scanned the smudged flight details on the whiteboard behind him. My flight had been delayed! I started to laugh.

At the departure gate, I sipped a McDonald's cappuccino and sat waiting, smiling.

CONTRIBUTOR BIOGRAPHIES

Sonja Bricker was born in San Francisco but raised in a small Navy town on the Kitsap Peninsula. After graduating with a degree in Spanish and English, she spent ten consecutive winters travelling in different countries, generally by bicycle. The other three seasons, she earned money by doing freelance magazine and newspaper work, plus many odd jobs. Eventually she returned to school for a Master's degree in Education and now teaches Spanish at the advanced level in a Seattle area high school. Last winter she spent two months cycling across Spain, conducting interviews with Spanish teens and producing short videos. Her work can be seen at spainwithsonja.blogspot.com.

Heather Conn travelled alone in India for seven months in 1990-91, which she describes in her memoir *No Letter in Your Pocket*. An author of three books, she has written for over fifty magazines, including *The Globe and Mail*, *The Vancouver Sun*, *Canadian Geographic* and *Sierra*. She wrote, produced and directed the documentary *A New Way: An Organic Garden Changes Lives* and has written for Bravo! and CBC Television. A freelance writer/editor, blogger and writing coach based in the Vancouver, B.C. region, Heather has an MFA in creative nonfiction writing from Goucher College in Baltimore, Maryland. See heatherconn.com for more info.

Jann Everard travelled in India as part of a year-long trip that also included climbing and trekking in Nepal and Tajikistan. Her short stories and creative nonfiction have been published in numerous Canadian and American journals, including *The Fiddlehead*, *The Dalhousie Review*, *The Los Angeles Review* **and** *Room*. Jann is currently working on a collection of short fiction. She lives in Toronto, where she works in health administration. Her website is www.janneverard.com.

Eufemia Fantetti is a graduate of Simon Fraser University's The Writer's Studio and holds an MFA in Creative Writing. She is a winner of *Event Magazine's* creative nonfiction contest and is a two-time finalist in the

Canadian National Playwriting competition. Her writing was listed with *Notable Essays of 2009* in *The Best American Essays Series* and her work recently won recognition in *Accenti Magazine* and the 2012 *Fish Anthology* short memoir contest. Her fiction, nonfiction and playwriting are included in the anthologies *Contours*, *Beyond Crazy* and *eye wuz here*. Mother Tongue Publishing will release her short story collection, *A Recipe for Disaster and Other Unlikely Tales of Love*, in November 2013. Visit eufemiafantetti.com for more info.

Farah Ghuznavi is a writer and newspaper columnist, with a professional background in development work. Her writing has been widely anthologized in the UK, US, Canada, Singapore, India, Nepal and her native Bangladesh. Her story "Judgement Day" was Highly Commended in the Commonwealth Short Story Competition 2010, and "Getting There" placed second in the Oxford GEF Competition, held at Oxford University and judged by the British novelist and *Guardian* newspaper columnist Bidisha. Farah was selected to be Writer in Residence for the Commonwealth Writers website, and has most recently edited the *Lifelines* anthology, published by Zubaan Books in India.

Janis Harper is a Vancouver writer, editor, actor and singer-song-writer who just completed her first CD, *Better This Way*. A long-time college and university writing instructor, she is currently transitioning out of teaching and into the field of expressive arts therapy. Janis has co-founded two local periodicals, published journalism and scholarship, and her literary prose and poetry have appeared in magazines and anthologies, including *Ars Medica*, *subTerrain*, *Reader's Digest*, *Room*, *CV 2*, *Tessera*, and *Lost on Purpose: Women in the City* (Seal Press, 2005). Her first anthology of creative nonfiction, which she conceived, edited and contributed to, is *Body Breakdowns: Tales of Illness and Recovery* (Anvil Press, 2007).

Vawn Himmelsbach is a Toronto-based journalist and travel writer who has spent more than three years travelling abroad, including a one-year stint as an English-language editor in China. Her travels have taken her from the cobblestone streets of old Tbilisi in Georgia to the Guge Kingdom in western Tibet to the ancient Mayan city of El Mirador in the jungles of northern Guatemala. She has written travel articles for a number of publications, including *CBC.ca, Metro News, Flare, Sweet Travel, Hotelier* and *Planeteye Traveler*, and contributed to a travel guidebook on China. She is also the co-founder of a travel website for women, called chicsavvytravels.com. In addition, she has written on topics ranging from martial arts to the latest tech gadgets for various print and online publications. She has been nominated for two journalism awards.

After working in India for several months as a journalist, **Denyse Johnson** relives her experience navigating the intoxicating culture through her short story "Good Business." Curious by nature, she has travelled to and worked in more than twenty countries where the people she meets and stories she collects are her favourite souvenirs. A former print and broadcast journalist, Denyse has been published in print and online magazines including *Winnipeg Women, Canadian Escapes, Oxygen* and *Inside Vancouver.ca*. She's completing her MA in International/Intercultural Communications through Royal Roads University.

K. Lorraine Kiidumae is an adjunct graduate of Simon Fraser University's The Writer's Studio, where she studied fiction with Shaena Lambert and Timothy Taylor. She is currently a creative writing mentor through the Vancouver School Board's Making Contact program and is working on completing her first novel. Her work has appeared in the 2011 and 2012 *emerge* anthologies, and "The Girl in the Grey Dress" was a winner in the Fraser Valley Writing School's 2012 literary competition. She shares her time between Vancouver and her home in Nanoose Bay.

Leanne Leduc is a registered emergency nurse who works and lives in North Vancouver. A wanderer at heart, she has travelled extensively in over forty countries, including a four-month journey through India. With the encouragement of family and friends, Leanne discovered a new passion in capturing her foreign adventures through writing. This is her first publication.

Bronwyn McBride's love affair with the Indian subcontinent culminated when she was twenty-one and moved to Mumbai to work with the educational nonprofit organization Atma, indulge in *idli sambar* and discover a *joie de vivre* in the most unlikely of circumstances. She catalogued the raw and heartbreaking beauty of the city in her blog, www.littlebirdbombay.com, and additionally contributed to a variety of travel and expat websites. She is currently studying infant cognitive development at Simon Fraser University in Vancouver and looks forward to her return to Mumbai.

Sarah Mian's debut novel, *When the Saints* will be published by HarperCollins in 2015. Her fiction and poetry have appeared in journals such as *The New Quarterly*, *subTerrain*, *The Antigonish Review*, *Galleon Journal*, *Filling Station* and *The Vagrant Revue of New Fiction*. She was a semi-finalist for CBC Canada Writes and a finalist for the Writers' Union of Canada Short Prose Competition. By day, Sarah works as an exhibit custodian in a forensic lab; by night, she writes at her little beach house in Queensland, Nova Scotia.

Margaret Miller has travelled widely over three decades in Australia, the Middle East, Europe and Central America. The inspiration for her story was a five-month journey to India in 2009-2010, where she volunteered for the environmental organization Navdanya. Her writing projects include academic editing at UBC and the Vancouver School of Theology and many, many letters. This is her first published story.

Ashlee Petrucci resides in Vancouver, B.C. She studied English literature and political science at the University of Calgary. A wanderlust for travel always tugs at her heartstrings, but for the moment she is content teaching ESL and dreaming of faraway worlds in reality and in writing. She is currently working on her first novel and hopes that Inspiration allows her to finish.

Beverley Reid is an award-winning filmmaker and writer living in the Gulf Islands of British Columbia. Her main interest is in telling stories from the developing world, and she has directed over twenty on-location documentaries in East Africa, India, Nepal, Central America, the Philippines and Southeast Asia. Her films have been honoured in many international festivals and broadcast in Canada and abroad. Beverley has extensive experience as a scriptwriter and is currently completing a nonfiction book, *Mango Dreams: Filmmaking Adventures in the Developing World*. She has also written two textbooks, a memoir and numerous articles. Her most memorable

Indian experiences include shooting in the slums of Kolkata and in isolated villages of the Himalayas.

Ulrike Rodrigues writes for the bicycle industry in Vancouver, B.C. In 2008, she bought and pedalled a one-speed Indian bicycle on the back roads that surround her grandparents' ancestral village near Porvorim, Goa. She wrote sixty stories about the six-month exploration for *Girl Gone Goa: Travel, Sex, and Magic in an Indian State* at girlgonegoa. wordpress.com. Ulrike has written for or been interviewed by *The Globe and Mail*, *Outpost*, *Momentum*, *Chatelaine* and CBC Radio. She contributed to *On Bicycles: 50 Ways the New Bike Culture can Change your Life*. See ulrike.ca for more info.

Born in Poona/Pune, India, **Renée Sarojini Saklikar** has lived in Newfoundland, Nova Scotia, Northern Ontario, Quebec, Saskatchewan and British Columbia. She writes *thecanadaproject*, a life-long poem chronicle. Work from *thecanadaproject* appears in literary journals and newspapers, including *The Vancouver Review*, *The Georgia Straight*, *Geist*, *subTerrain*, *Poetry is Dead*, *CV2*, and *Arc Poetry Magazine* and in the recent anthologies, *Alive at the Center: Contemporary Poems from the Pacific Northwest* and *Force Field: 77 Women Poets of British Columbia*. The first completed series from *the canada project*, a book-length sequence of elegies, *children of air india*, about Canada and the bombing of Air India Flight 182, is forthcoming from Nightwood Editions.

Leah Sherry is a media literacy high school teacher in Toronto. She lived and worked in Kolkata, India, from 1998-2001. In 2006, Leah self-published a collection of short stories and poetry titled *Warm Ups*. In 2009, she returned to Kolkata to reunite with her friends and community there. When Leah returned to Toronto, she wrote a screenplay based on her experiences. Leah currently lives in Toronto and hopes to complete her MFA in Creative Writing. Her life and work in Kolkata continues to be one of the greatest experiences of her life.

Morelle Smith is a freelance writer, editor and translator. She has published several books of poetry and fiction, including *Time Loop* and *The Way Words Travel*. Her work has appeared in many magazines and anthologies, such as *New Writing Scotland, The Dublin Quarterly, Times Literary Supplement, Ljubljana Tales* and *La Traductière*. Based in Scotland, she has been awarded six Writers Residencies in France and Switzerland, and her work has been translated into French, Albanian, Bulgarian and Romanian. Her travels have taken her through the Balkans, Turkey, Iran, Afghanistan and India. Her degree is in English and French literature, and her blog is Rivertrain. blogspot.com.

Liz Snell studied writing at the University of Victoria. She travelled throughout India and lived in New Delhi for nine months. While there, she homeschooled for two expat families and volunteered at a school for slum children. She currently lives in Victoria, B.C.

Jill "Janaki" Stock's many travels to India to study and teach yoga over fourteen years, as well as her background as an artist, have given her a rich creative foundation. She is currently exploring consciousness and cultural identity through drawing a comic strip called *Becoming Sita*. Jill is also merging her two passions, yoga and art, by writing a book about the aspect of symbol in Hatha yoga.

Kathryn Sutton is a writer whose work has appeared in publications in Canada, England and New Zealand, and in the food and drink guide *Bar Secrets Vancouver*. As well as travel features, she specializes in long-form articles on fields ranging from health sciences to Bollywood. When she isn't travelling the globe, she lives in Vancouver, B.C., with her husband and son.

Lauren Van Mullem is a freelance writer and Southern California native who specializes in crafting words about food, travel and small businesses. As co-owner of CopyMuse.com, she spends most of her time clacking away at her laptop, but when she gets up, it's to cook, hike, take pictures or take the first step of her next journey. Lauren's work can be found on WanderlustandLipstick.com, PeterGreenberg. com and the *Santa Barbara Independent* newspaper, among other places. Her bangle from the night train to Varanasi sits on her writing desk.

Mariken Van Nimwegen, originally from the Netherlands, has lived in Vancouver since 1977 and worked for the *Vancouver Sun* newspaper for twenty years as an editorial illustrator and graphic designer. She wrote a column for the same paper, called "Culture Seen," that described the cultures and religions of immigrant communities from all over the world that reside in Vancouver. She attended the Academy of Fine Arts in Rotterdam, Holland, has a BA in anthropology from UBC and a Master's in Liberal Studies from SFU. She has travelled to six continents and continues to visit the world's most amazing nooks and crannies, often solo.

Jennifer Waescher is a Canadian writer and musician who has been residing in Seoul, South Korea, for the last several years. In addition to living abroad, she has travelled extensively in Asia, including one nine-month journey, which included several months in India. She is also a published children's storywriter in Seoul, with a series of illustrated children's stories. Other Seoul publications include travel articles in *Groove Magazine* and prose and poetry in several English literary magazines. She also writes regular articles for her co-founded webzine. Jennifer is delighted to be included in this anthology, her first Canadian publication. For more information, writing and music, please see www.jenniferwaescher.com.

Jasmine Yen spent two months in 2010 travelling on her own and with her brother in India. She fell in love with the country and sent emails detailing her travels to her friends and family. These emails reached Janis Harper, who invited Jasmine to contribute to this book. This is her first publication. When she's not exploring exotic destinations, Jasmine lives in Vancouver, B.C.

Jennifer Zickerman is a Vancouver-based writer and editor who has had the good fortune to travel extensively both for pleasure and business. Her piece in this anthology is drawn from a journal written in 1999 when she backpacked solo around India, Nepal and Thailand for nine months. She is a professional technical writer and editor interested in open source software technologies and also blogs on various topics (particularly ecology, organic gardening and neighbour-hood development) at www.jenzed.com, www.farmtoforkherbs.ca and www.hammondneighbours.ca.